THE THIRD BOOK IN A SERIES COVERING ALL ASPECTS OF B

ALAN H. FAULKNER

THE GEORGE & THE MARY
A HISTORY OF THE GRAND UNION CANAL CARRYING COMPANY LTD

An unidentified GUCCC pair ascending Bascote Double Lock (Tony Smith)

Nine pairs of boats, mainly from the Associated Canal Carriers fleet, in Regent's Canal Dock awaiting loading (or clearance). At the time Roland Argo Wharves Limited, an Anglo-German company, operated many of the wharves around the dock. (Tony Smith)

On 1 January 1929 the Grand Union Canal Company came into being as a result of the Regent's Canal & Dock Company acquiring four other companies and bringing the canal route from the Regent's Canal Dock at Limehouse and from Brentford, both on the river Thames, to Birmingham and Leicester under the same management for the first time. Three years later a further three companies were acquired taking the canal line northwards from Leicester down the river Soar and up the river Erewash valley to Langley Mill in Nottinghamshire.

The new company quickly set about improving its route but at the same time it realised that new traffic would not follow automatically but would have to be actively sought and competed for. Even before the 1929 merger it had started laying the grounds as to how this could be achieved.

George & Mary: On 20 July 1928 the-then Regent's Canal & Dock Company had accepted a tender from the Steel Barrel Co. Ltd. of Uxbridge to build a pair of narrow boats intended to be used for carrying between London and Birmingham. Their design had been approved by Bernard Ives, who was naval architect to the Regent's company. The Uxbridge concern had tendered £473 for a steel motorboat and £386 for a steel butty boat, both with wooden cabins to be built and fitted by Bushell Brothers of Tring. Meanwhile Perman & Company had agreed to supply a single-cylinder 22hp-Kromhout marine oil engine with equipment and installation for a total of £307. After providing another £41 for tarpaulins and making an offsetting £30 allowance for fitting the engine the total cost was £1,177.25.

The new pair was delivered in February 1929, the motor being named GEORGE and the butty MARY after King George V (1910-1936) and his queen Mary. Both were somewhat larger than the usual narrow boat with an improved and modernised design that was intended for them to be able to navigate out onto the river Thames.

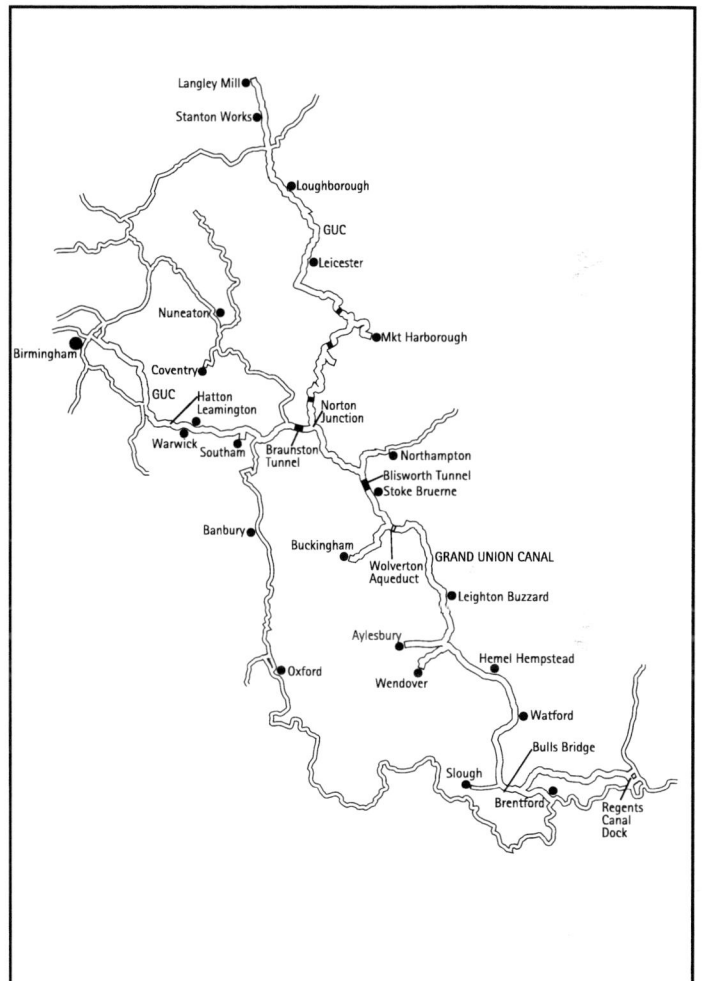

The motor boat GEORGE, which was a forerunner for what was to become the large GUCCC fleet, was designed by a naval architect, was built at Uxbridge and entered service in February 1929. GEORGE is shown here approaching Cotton End, Northampton where Associated Canal Carriers initially based. For much of the time in carrying service GEORGE was run by the Bevington family. (The Waterways Archive, Gloucester)

Arthur Harvey-Taylor, a carrier based at Aylesbury, agreed to take the boats from 1 April 1929 for an initial six month free trial period during which he would be able to test the boats thoroughly and evaluate their carrying capacity. The intention was that he would then acquire the boats on hire purchase terms over five years.

Several of his captains operated the boats but they all experienced problems. For instance when loading bagged wheat men standing at the bottom of the holds found the sides were so tall they could not reach out and transfer the bags from the barge. Despite this, sixty tons of wheat were loaded at Brentford for Aylesbury whilst a return cargo was sixty-six tons of silver sand from Garsides pit at Leighton Buzzard.

When there was a good depth of water in the canal it was said no boat could catch the pair, not even the mill dashers that operated express services between John Dickinson & Co. Ltd's mills in Hertfordshire and its London depot. When the depth was restricted, however, as was often the case, the pair could only crawl along. The trial period was later extended to the end of December 1929 but Harvey-Taylor eventually decided not to purchase the boats.

Associated Canal Carriers: In 1930 Associated Canal Carriers Ltd. (ACC), a small carrying company based at Northampton, found itself in financial difficulties. It had been formed on 28 January 1929 when the firm Midland Canal Transport became a limited company and it ran a fleet of six horse-drawn boats - DOROTHY, DOVE, OWL, ROOK, SALLY, TARZAN - and the motor boat, HAWK. The chairman was D. J. Hamilton Lister who held 10,000 of the 20,000 founders shares of 25p each with Charles Payne Crofts and L. V. James as joint managing directors each holding 5,000 founders shares.

The company occupied the Grand Union's wharf and warehouse

MARY, GEORGE's butty, shown on the approach to the Northampton Depot. MARY was never numbered into the GUCCC fleet but was withdrawn at an early date and became a maintenance boat. (The Waterways Archive, Gloucester)

at Northampton, which had originally been leased to Payne Crofts and James in 1925 and it was also represented at Brentford and Birmingham. Partly owing to severe weather conditions early in 1929 when boats were frozen in for many weeks and the goods had to be sent by road, ACC incurred a loss in its first year to the 28 February 1930 and matters were not helped by the bankruptcy of Hamilton Lister soon after.

This led to the other directors approaching the Grand Union and at its board meeting on 13 August 1930 it decided to go ahead and purchase ACC for £750 whilst writing off a further £609 that was already owed for tolls. This involved paying 9d (4p) for each of the 20,000 founder's shares, agreeing to continue ACC's business and taking on its entire staff. The takeover took place in October when the Grand Union appointed Wilfred Curtis, Ernest Woolley and Christopher Tatham as directors whilst Payne Crofts was retained as the company's agent in Northampton.

It was not long before ACC's new owners started to expand the small fleet. In November 1930 the motorboat ARETHUSA and its butty PROSPERITY were acquired from John Walker of Bugbrooke for £360, the motorboat being renamed ADVANCE. Tonnages were still fairly modest with 705 tons being handled in October 1930, 463 tons in November and 557 tons in December with the principal cargoes being coal, grain and sugar.

The Royalty Class: In January 1931 ACC agreed to hire GEORGE & MARY from the Grand Union for £1.50 per week but this was reduced to £1 per week in May as the boats were still being used at times for test purposes. Based on the experience of operating the pair, tenders were invited in February for the construction of some new boats of similar design and in March the following orders were placed.

1: W. J. Yarwood & Sons Ltd. of Northwich to build four motorboat hulls with plates of copper-bearing steel, two for £588 each and two

With the widening of the locks on the Warwick Canals between Napton and Birmingham, a wide boat named "PROGRESS" was built at Bushell Brothers' Tring boatyard to see how well she would travel through the new locks and on up to Birmingham. She was launched in the autumn of 1934 and was first used to take the Duke of Kent and other invited guests to the official opening of the new locks at Hatton on 30 October. In service it was found she did not travel well as the channel widening works could not be completed before the money ran out. Instead she was used on the southern section of the Grand Union before being transferred to the company's maintenance fleet. (The Waterways Archive, Gloucester)

for £595 each.
2: James Pollock Sons & Co. Ltd. of Faversham - two steel hulls for £948 each with 20hp Bolinder engines installed.
3: W. H. Walker & Brothers Ltd. of Rickmansworth - two wooden butties for £340 each.
4: Edward George Woods of Brentford - two wooden butties for £330 each.
5: Bushell Brothers of Tring - two wooden butties for £380 each.
6: Two 18/21hp 450 rpm Petter engines for £272 each for two of the Yarwood hulls.
7: One 22hp 440 rpm Kromhout engine for £345 and one 18/21hp 600 rpm twin cylinder Kromhout engine for £290 for the other two Yarwood hulls.

The first boat delivered was DUCHESS in June 1931 from Edward Woods and the rest followed at intervals, the orders being completed with WILLIAM from Yarwoods in April 1932. The boats were similar to GEORGE & MARY and were named DUKE & DUCHESS; EDWARD & ALEXANDRA (after Edward VII [1901-1910] and his queen Alexandra); HENRY & ANNE (after Henry VIII [1509-1547] and Anne Boleyn); PRINCE & PRINCESS, VICTORIA & ALBERT (after Queen Victoria [1837-1901] and her consort Prince Albert); and WILLIAM & ADELAIDE (after William IV [1830-1837] and Queen Adelaide) thus comprising what became known as the Royalty Class.

ACC also expanded its fleet by continuing to purchase boats

EDWARD & ALEXANDRA and *HENRY & ANNE* awaiting loading in Regent's Canal Dock with another two pairs ahead of them. (The Waterways Archive, Gloucester)

from other carriers. The motor JOSEPHINE MARGUERITE came from Rupert Craven of Faringdon for £215 in November 1932 together with its butty COOMBE ABBEY for £80, but over £90 then had to be spent on repairing the engine and repainting the boats. Early in 1933 the butty RUGBY was bought from Fellows, Morton & Clayton Ltd. of Birmingham for £85 to work with the motor HAWK. Another motor, SPEEDY, came from Rupert Craven in February 1934 for £224 and soon after the butty SHAMROCK was purchased from John G. Grantham of Banbury for £95 to work with it. Then two horse boats - COUNT and COUNTESS - came from Bells United Asbestos Co. Ltd. of Harefield for £114 each and early in January 1935 DORNEY COURT & ELSIE EDITH were bought from John Brookes of Bedworth for £450.

Meanwhile most of ACC's old horse boats had been disposed of in December 1931 when DOROTHY and ROOK were sold to the Grand Union parent company for £80 whilst DOVE, SALLIE and TARZAN were given away. The last boat, OWL, was sold for £25 early in 1933. By early 1934 there were eleven motors and thirteen butties in service, but the only survivor from the original ACC fleet was the motor HAWK.

On 12 March 1934 ACC launched a much more ambitious expansion programme with the first objective being to increase the fleet up to 100 pairs of boats. To this end the company's name was changed to the Grand Union Canal Carrying Company Ltd. (GUCCC) and the capital was doubled to £20,000. The move coincided with the impending completion of the work of widening the locks on the canal between Napton and Birmingham and the stepping up of the drive for new traffics where one early success had been granite chippings from Nuneaton in Warwickshire to the London area.

Several pairs of GUCCC boats alongside what is now the popular Waterways Museum at Stoke Bruerne. This was a regular tying-up place and even more so as Sister Mary Ward was based in one of the canal side cottages and tended to the boat people's health and welfare. In 1951 she was awarded the British Empire Medal in recognition of her work. (The Waterways Archive, Gloucester.

CODES: A.B.C. 5TH EDITION AND BOE.

GRAND UNION CANAL CARRYING CO., LTD.

TELEPHONE:
ROYAL 5630 (10 LINES)

TELEGRAPHIC ADDRESS:
CANALISE, FEN,
LONDON.

DIRECTORS:
E.J. WOOLLEY
JOHN MILLER
J.M. WHITTINGTON
W.K. SIMPSON
R.H. MOLL

PORT OF LONDON BUILDING, SEETHING LANE,
LONDON, E.C.3

OUR REF. RHM/W/W.

YOUR REF.

The letter heading of the Grand Union Canal Carrying Company, which was used from April 1937 up to the outbreak of the Second World War when most of the offices were moved out to Ruislip. (Author's collection)

The Star Class: Tenders were invited for building some wooden boats and two pairs were ordered from Harland & Wolff Ltd. (H&W) of Woolwich, one pair from Edward Woods at £655, one pair from Walkers at £800, and one pair from Nurser Brothers of Braunston for £695. The H&W boats were to be built to drawings prepared by H. S. Jespersen and by Bushell Brothers, Jespersen soon after being appointed the GUCCC's Engineer and Naval Architect on a salary of £400.

Nursers were unable to carry out their order; instead a second pair was ordered from Walkers at £800 and another from Woods at £655. Later Woods also had to forego producing this second pair and to replace it Walkers agreed to build a third pair. Six Russell Newbery 18hp diesel engines were purchased for £216 each for the motorboats. From 1 June 1934 Leslie Morton was appointed as manager of the fleet on a salary of £500 and Richard Moll was appointed company secretary at £200 from 15 June.

The first pair to be delivered was ARCTURUS & SIRIUS from Walkers in October 1934 to be followed in December by NEPTUNE & ALTAIR from the same builders, VENUS & SATURN from H&W and JUPITER & MARS from Woods. ALDEBARAN & ORION arrived from H&W in January 1935, whilst Gaumont British News filmed the launch of the sixth pair, ANTARES & SPICA, from Walkers on 18 February. These six pairs became the forerunners of the Star Class, so called because most of the craft were named after stars and constellations. The class eventually numbered eighty-eight pairs.

These prototypes were followed by larger orders. In January 1935 twenty-four pairs of composite boats, with iron sides and elm bottoms, were ordered from H&W for £1,275 per pair complete with National diesel engines together with twelve pairs of similar craft but with Russell Newbery engines from Yarwoods at £1,250 per pair

W. J. Yarwood & Sons Ltd., shipbuilders at Northwich, built four of the original Royalty Class motor boats and the third, EDWARD, is shown outside the yard shortly after her launch on 16 November 1931. She left Northwich a week later en route to Northampton. (Author's collection)

and six pairs of wooden boats with oak sides and elm bottoms from Walkers at £790 per pair which excluded the cost of the Russell Newbery engines.

Yet more orders were placed in May 1935; eighteen pairs from H&W with mild steel sides, elm bottoms and National diesels at £1,276 per pair, eight pairs of all steel craft with "Vee" bottoms and Russell Newbery engines from Yarwoods at £1,301 per pair, twelve pairs from Walkers similar to the first batch but with National engines and costing £1,128 per pair, and two pairs from Woods with National engines at £1,006 per pair.

Deliveries of the first batch of H&W boats - known as the Little Woolwich Class - started in May 1935 with THEMIS & TITANIA and HYPERION & HYADES to be completed in October with PLANET & NEBULAE. The second batch followed on immediately with ACHERNAR & ACTIS and was completed in December with DORADO & RIGAL.

Deliveries from Yarwoods - the Little Northwich Class - started in May with PISCES & PUPPIS and were completed in January 1936 with ANTLIA & LUPUS whilst the second batch - the Middle Northwich Class - was started in November 1935 with RADIANT & REGULUS and was completed in June 1936 with ZODIAC & LEONIDS.

Production of the Little Ricky Class from Walkers averaged about a pair a month beginning with CASTOR & POLLUX in April 1935 and finishing with ORPHEUS & PHAETHON in June 1936, the last boat from Woods also arriving in that month.

The Star Class boats were 71ft 6in long, 7ft 0½in wide with a draught of 3ft 3in. Their holds were 4ft 2in deep, which gave the boats considerably more freeboard than usual, thus enabling them to work safely in tidal estuaries. The Middle Northwich boats had 4ft 6in holds but the Royalty Class had holds no less than 4ft 11in deep, which made then rather cumbersome. Compared to the traditional narrow boat of the time the new boats were of an improved design as was fitting for the modern transport system the GUCCC was trying to create.

To finance this expansion the parent Grand Union Company had contributed more share capital increasing this up to £30,000 and as part of this the original 20,000 founders shares of 25p each were consolidated into 5,000 ordinary £1 shares. Then in June 1935 the London Stock Exchange gave permission for the issue of £120,000

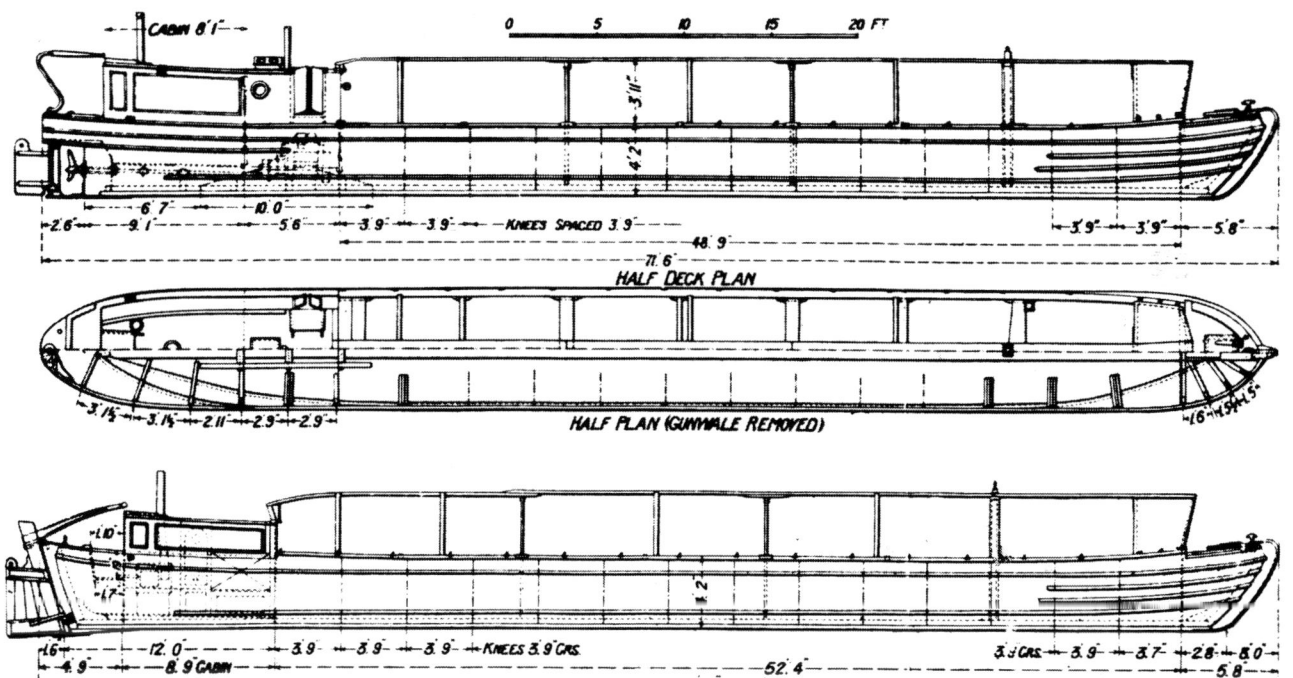

of a 6% income debenture stock and the Premier Investment Company took this up in full.

Bulls Bridge Depot: Initially it seems the fleet was based at Brentford but as it grew in size plans had to be made for the setting up of a proper depot and a site owned by the Grand Union was selected at Bulls Bridge, where the Paddington branch joined the main line from Brentford. Eventually the facilities extended from Bulls Bridge Dock, sometimes called the Weigh Dock, that was almost opposite the junction over 350 yards eastwards to the site of Mead's Dock, a barge repair dock occupied by William Iszard Ltd.

Initially the GUCCC rented a modest 2,300 square yards and in January 1935 it was estimated a fuel depot and repair shop would cost £1,067. The Grand Union started on the work soon after, the site being levelled by April when a contract was let for the buildings. Shortly after a storekeeper was appointed at the new depot and a fleet superintendent followed in August. Further buildings such as

CLYPEUS & CORVUS were built by Yarwoods and are shown here immediately prior to leaving the Northwich yard on 6 June 1935 to start their journey south. They were the second pair in the "Small Northwich" Class. (Cheshire County Council)

a repair shop were erected and by the summer of 1936 additional land was needed with work on the erection of new offices starting in December. Meanwhile Bulls Bridge Dock had been converted into a dry dock and roofed over. In January 1937 Edwin Wood was appointed manager of the depot and he remained in charge for many years.

In February 1937 the GUCCC applied to construct a 650-feet long lay-by set back by 52-feet from the canal bank so that six boats could lie abreast without obstructing the canal. The company also asked to take over the tenancy of Iszard's dock, which was due to expire in the following month. Both requests went ahead although it was soon decided the boats should lie head on in the lay-by rather than abreast.

In March 1937 the construction of a covered side slipway was authorised and by the beginning of March 1938 this was virtually complete as were shops for the sail makers and blacksmiths together with a recreation hut. A second side slip was authorised in June 1938 and later in that year machinery formerly installed at Iszard's Dock was transferred to the carpenter's machine shop near this second slipway and several of Iszard's staff were taken on at the depot. In November 1938 a new store was erected where top and side cloths could be dressed and stored and later washhouses and showers were installed for the boatmen to use. The depot was capable of dealing with any kind of repair so as to keep the growing fleet in service.

All the work on the depot was financed by the Grand Union and up to the end of June 1937 it had invested £6,115. The GUCCC had to pay a charge of 4% on this capital sum by way of rent for the various facilities.

In July 1936 the company purchased Hugh Sephton's boatyard at Sutton Stop, Hawkesbury, on the Coventry Canal for £410 but it seems to have made little use of the facility.

In April 1936 the GUCCC chairman, reporting on this massive expansion said

"Never before in the history of Canal Transport has such a programme been embarked upon. The greater the number of boats in commission, the more economically and efficiently we can run our concern."

The Town Class: Indeed, even before the delivery of the Star Class boats had been completed contracts were placed for still more craft and by March 1936 another eighty-six pairs were on order. These comprised twenty-four pairs of craft with both steel sides and steel bottoms from H&W with National diesels at £1,363.25 per pair; a further twenty-four motor boats of the same design from H&W at £900 each; thirty-eight all-steel motors fitted with National engines from Yarwoods at £900 and sixty-two wooden butties from Walkers at £390 each. In the event six of the Yarwood motors - OAKLEY, PADDINGTON, READING, RENTON, SOUTHALL, STAMFORD - were fitted with Russell Newbery engines.

The first arrivals from H&W - known as the Big Woolwich Class

London City Missions opened a Boatmen's Institute at The Butts, Brentford in December 1904 close to the canal to provide for the families working on the Grand Union. In October 1945 Mr. F. J Chapman took over as missionary and he continued in this role until his retirement in July 1972. He is shown here talking to the boat lady on ROADE. (Robert Wilson collection)

The GUCCC fleet was based at a purpose-built depot at Bulls Bridge that was equipped with full facilities to maintain the fleet and this shows two of the slipways and a cluster of the company's boats. The entrance to the Paddington Branch is on the right. (Tony Smith)

- came in July 1936 with the completion of ABER & ALPERTON and the motor BARROW. Two other single motors were finished soon after but the builders concentrated primarily on the pairs, which were finished in December with BUCKDEN & BUDE. The building of the motors then started in earnest, the order being completed in May 1937 with HAWKESBURY.

HALSALL was the first motor from Yarwoods in the Big Northwich Class arriving at the end of June 1936 and the batch was completed with YEOFORD in April 1937. Deliveries from Walkers in the Big Ricky Class started at the end of June 1936 with HALTON. Thereafter production averaged four per month until September 1937 when deliveries started to tail off and the last boats, HAGLEY and HALE, did not arrive until towards the end of 1938.

All these boats were of very similar design to the Star Class but had holds 4ft 9½in deep and they were known as the Town Class being named after towns and villages in the British Isles. The high-speed diesel engines were designed to give a loaded speed of six knots, whilst the pairs were intended to carry 72 tons on a draught of 4ft 3in. In practice the dredged depth of the canals rarely permitted this maximum to be achieved; the highest recorded tonnage on a pair was 63¼ tons of wheat from Brentford to Wellingborough aboard BUCKDEN & BRIGHTON.

During the war several all female crews were recruited to take the place of men called up to serve in the forces. Here a group of them are shown at the lay-by at Bulls Bridge with their trainer, Kit Gayford, on the left. She was awarded an MBE for her work. (Hugh McKnight)

With the delivery of the Town Class the GUCCC had one of the largest fleets of long-distance narrow boats in the country and the boats were given special numbers, the motors running from 1 to 186 and the butties from 201 to 387, there being an extra butty from the old ACC days. Initially the butties were numbered with their respective motorboat's number and the suffix "B", thus HEBE, which worked with the motor ISIS, was originally 54B before being given its final number of 290.

The GUCCC also had its own classification system.
Type A - the original Royalty Class pair GEORGE & MARY
Type B - the other six Royalty Class pairs
Type C - the six prototype Star Class pairs
Type D - the seventy-four standard Star Class pairs
Type E - the eight "Vee" bottom Middle Northwich pairs
Type F - the eighty-six Town Class pairs

ARGUS and her motor boat northbound in Ironbridge Lock No 77 at Watford on 19 June 1932. The picture was taken from the bridge across the tail of the lock, a favourite spot for photographers. (Hertfordshire County Council)

Extra funding was now needed and up to £130,000 of a new 6% mortgage debenture stock was issued. To provide the lenders with more security for this, the Grand Union subscribed for another 100,000 £1 ordinary shares, albeit initially these were only 12½p paid up, the intention being for the GUCCC to make further calls as the need arose.

The Drive for Traffics: Coupled with this vigorous expansion policy was a concerted drive to secure more trade both for the fleet and for the canal. Rather than taking existing cargoes off other canal carriers most of the company's traffic was secured in fair competition from rail and road. Probably the most important was iron and steel, much being won from the railways.

On 14 October 1935 the steam ship DONA ISABEL arrived in the Regent's Canal Dock from Ghent in Belgium and discharged 1,250 tons of iron and steel into a fleet of over twenty pairs of narrow boats for delivery to Birmingham and the South Staffordshire area. Initially this development led to a major dispute with the railway companies who claimed it breached agreement on rates, but the company persisted and the traffic became a regular feature at the dock. Canal transport often saved up to four days in delivery times and cost about 13½p per ton less.

Other traffics secured included leather waste from Northampton to Limehouse with last blocks as return loading from the docks; cresylic acid from the docks to Birmingham with zinc ashes as return loading, bulk cheese from the docks to Aylesbury with processed cheese as return loading, and non-ferrous metals from the docks to Deanshanger on the Buckingham branch albeit this was short-lived.

Another innovation, established in 1935, was a shuttle service of craft from the Rugby Portland Cement Company's works at Southam to Sampson Road in Birmingham. Automatic loading and unloading facilities were installed at Southam and Birmingham under cover

The motor boat USWORTH and its butty leaving the fifth lock down in the Hatton flight on their way north to Birmingham. Hatton workshops and depot are on the right. (The Waterways Archive, Gloucester)

As an experiment a cargo of small cars was loaded onto a pair of narrow boats in Birmingham and delivered to Brentford Depot. The picture shows motor BALDOCK being unloaded. (Robert Wilson Collection)

and about 2,000 tons of cement per month was transported. The service was a great success and showed the GUCCC a good profit whilst reducing cement bag breakages to nil.

Large tonnages of grain were secured, loading from ships in the London docks for delivery to various mills and warehouses along the canal. The new boats, which had a capacity of 2,800 cubic feet below gunwales all of which was protected from the weather by tarpaulins, made it possible to carry most of the grain in bulk, as opposed to in sacks as was usually the case before. This cut out the expense of bagging, sack hire, emptying the sacks and returning the empties. Strawboards, both in bundles and reels, were handled from Regent's Canal Dock to Northampton, Coventry, Birmingham and Nuneaton. Much of this traffic had to be warehoused, sorted and then delivered over a period of time to the customer's requirements.

All classes of timber were handled, mainly for delivery to the Midlands. It was either transhipped from lighters at Brentford or loaded direct from ships in Regent's Canal Dock. Large tonnages of coal and smaller tonnages of road stone were handled from the Warwickshire collieries and quarries. To control this traffic an office was established at Hawkesbury Junction, near Coventry as early as

October 1935 and the company was in daily contact with the pits in connection with the placing and loading of the boats.

One of the most important contracts for the carriage of coal was secured in 1938 for the exclusive supply of John Dickinson & Co. Ltd's mills at Apsley, Nash and Croxley in Hertfordshire. This, however, was a cut-rate offer acquired at the expense of the consortium of owner boatmen who had previously supplied most of the mills requirements. Another traffic handled was sand from the various pits alongside the canal, such as at Leighton Buzzard, destined for the London area whilst much general cargo was dealt with mainly on the London to Birmingham route.

Trading position: The effect of all this in terms of tonnage carried and tolls paid to the Grand Union is shown in this table: -

Year	Tonnage	Tolls	Year	Tonnage	Tolls
1931	8,999	£1,063	1937	168,430	£17,470
1932	13,694	1,189	1938	179,733	17,553
1933	14,849	1,570	1939	165,490	16,782
1934	25,283	2,126	1940	152,670	21,031
1935	56,026	4,718	1941	168,638	29,946
1936	142,460	13,440			

There was a severe frost in January & February 1940.

In terms of traffic gained for the canal the expansion programme was a success, but in other respects it was a disaster. The loss on the carrying side peaked at nearly £32,000 in 1937 as the heavy charges for depreciation on the new boats and the £15,000 debenture interest had to be met. Thereafter the loss started to reduce with a small profit even being earned in 1941 and later the company was aided by a government wartime subsidy.

A cluster of GUCCC boats awaiting unloading in the side arm at Sampson Road Depot. (The Waterways Archive, Gloucester)

A busy scene at Sampson Road Depot with several pairs unloading. As part of its development programme the Grand Union invested in transforming existing wharves here into a modern inland port. The work included a new warehouse with a branch canal running right into the building. The Lord Mayor of Birmingham officially opened the new depot on 27 September 1938. (The Waterways Archive, Gloucester)

The GUCCC maintained depots at Bulls Bridge, Bulbourne, Gayton, Hatton and Kilby Bridge from where boatmen could summon assistance in the event of difficulties. Here the service van has been called out to attend to problems in MEROPE's engine room. (The Waterways Archive, Gloucester)

Year	Loss	Cumulative	Year	Loss	Cumulative
28 Feb 1935	£2,895	£8,638	30 Nov 1941	+£1,837	£147,125
31 Dec 1935	18,198	26,836	31 Dec 1942	11,927	159,052
31 Dec 1936	25,576	52,412	31 Dec 1943	7,572	166,624
31 Dec 1937	31,960	84,372	31 Dec 1944	5,179	171,803
30 Nov 1938	26,863	111,235	31 Dec 1945	+13,827	157,976
30 Nov 1939	23,226	134,461	31 Dec 1946	+27,233	130,473
30 Nov 1940	14,501	148,962	31 Dec 1947	10,435	141,178

A Government subsidy of £24,900 was paid in 1946.

The factor that upset the company's plan mostly seems to have been the difficulty in finding crews for the craft. The total fleet in service never rose above the figure of 119 pairs achieved in September 1937 and this meant that much of the fleet was tied up idle. But even idle boats were still a heavy charge against profits through debenture interest and depreciation.

At the end of 1936 an internal disagreement within the GUCCC over the expansion brought about several management changes. On 27 October 1936 John Miller was appointed as a director of the GUCCC and on 12 November he became its new managing director. He decided that for the time being it would be the company's policy to work only 100 pairs of boats and to lay the remainder up in Stockley Dock. All the old boats were to be withdrawn from commission and only those in perfect working order were to be used but as and when required boats were to be brought back into service. In practice the limit on working numbers was not strictly adhered to, the company continuing to operate as many pairs as the crewing

The motor boat STAVERTON and its butty CHISWICK are being unloaded of their cargo of strawboards at Cotton End Wharf in Northampton. The cargo, which was one of the new traffics secured for the waterways, was stored in the warehouse pending delivery to the customer. (The Waterways Archive, Gloucester)

situation allowed.

As a result of this disagreement the manager Leslie Morton resigned, he being paid £1,000 in compensation in February 1937. His chairman, Wilfred Henry Curtis who had been behind the initial takeover of the Grand Junction Canal by the Regent's in 1929 and who had had the vision of the improved Warwick Line and the build up of the GUCCC fleet, followed him on 13 April 1937. Curtis had set his heart on making the company a success and it was a major disappointment to him to leave before this was achieved. Ernest John Woolley now took over as Chairman and several staff, such as Jespersen, the naval architect, and Moll, the secretary, were transferred over onto the Grand Union's payroll.

By March 1937 almost seventy pairs were laid up either in Stockley Dock or in the disused Cumberland Market Basin on the Regent's Canal. In July 1937, by when negotiations were in progress to legally abandon and infill the basin, all the boats there had to be moved to Stockley. In November 1938 it was decided that all the laid-up boats were to be moved to William Boyer & Sons gravel pit at Harefield and the last ones left Stockley on 14 April 1939. Many were to remain at Harefield for several years.

Before the GUCCC launched its expansion programme considerable doubts had been expressed in some quarters about the difficulties that were likely to arise. These included the problems of getting the new boats built, obtaining new traffics, finding new crews and, if the other snags could be overcome, dealing with the congestion that was likely to arise and the shortage of water over the watersheds. In practice finding suitable crews was the only serious problem.

Negotiations had been opened with the Ministry of Labour as early as September 1937 to try and overcome this problem by establishing a training centre for new boatmen. The outbreak of the Second World War only aggravated the shortage as many steerers were called up but by April 1941 a "Training Scheme for Canal Steerers" had been set up with four boatmen specially allocated to teach the new recruits. The training work proved unpopular and later was taken over by several women who went on to serve with distinction. In July 1944 there were three trainers – Miss Gayford with BATTERSEA & UTTOXETER, Miss French with CAPRICORN & CLEOPATRA and Miss Hall Smith with ASCOT & CRATER; Eily Gayford being awarded an M.B.E in the 1945 New Year's Honours List for this work. Several all-female crews were recruited, some of which served until the end of the hostilities.

In retrospect it is now obvious that the expansion plans were too ambitious, mainly because of the shortage of crews. A more modest scheme would have been just as successful in terms of traffic gained and would have showed a reasonable financial return. During the expansion period consideration was given to taking over the fleet of boats operated by S. E. Barlow of Tamworth. Talks started in July 1936 at which time Barlow was operating mainly coal contracts from the Warwickshire collieries to destinations on the Grand Union, notably to John Dickinson's Home Park Mill near Kings Langley in Hertfordshire. Negotiations were broken off in November as part of the change of policy by the new management.

The Erewash Company: When the Grand Union acquired the three navigations north of Leicester in 1932 it became the owner of two small carrying fleets that had been started by the Loughborough and Erewash concerns a few years before and were operated as a joint undertaking from an office at Loughborough. In March 1932 the Grand Union incorporated the Erewash Canal Carrying Co. Ltd., (ECCC) as a sister company to ACC, to continue these businesses. ECCC started out with fourteen horse boats, the new carrying

A pair of GUCCC boats is dwarfed by the bows of a sea-going ship as they load drums in Regent's Canal Dock. (The Waterways, Archive, Gloucester)

Three Stothert & Pitt luffing cranes tower over the butty TIVERTON at Tyseley Wharf in Birmingham. The wharf was developed as the main destination for the metal cargoes, such as steel, spelter and aluminium that were imported through Regent's Canal Dock. (Author's collection)

business being valued at £4,440 as a going concern, with its base moved to Leicester.

In line with the expansion of ACC, the Grand Union decided on a modest expansion of its Erewash fleet, resulting in an order being placed with Yarwoods in February 1935 for two pairs of iron composite boats estimated at £2,440. The boats were of very similar design to the Star Class and were named after trees, following the style of some of the earlier boats in the fleet. ELM & ASH were delivered on 9 August 1935 and CYPRUS & CEDAR followed on 26 September, the total cost coming to £2,507. The boats were one-foot shorter than those being built for the GUCCC to enable them to pass through Bishops Meadow Lock on the Loughborough Cut more easily.

Whilst some second hand boats had also been acquired, traffic demands were such that in June 1937 CASTOR & POLLUX were hired from the GUCCC to boost capacity. Initially the GUCCC wanted to charge the ECCC an annual £126 per pair and £26 per butty but this level was quickly reduced and by 1940 was £37.50 and £10 respectively. The GUCCC motors ACHERNAR, CASTOR, FOMALHAUT, LACERTA, MONOCEROS, OAKLEY, ORPHEUS, THEMIS and butties ACHILLES, ALTAIR, BETELGEUSE, CORVUS, DUBHE, GLAXY, MARS, MEDUSA, MILKY WAY, POLLUX, RUISLIP, SATURN were the most regular ones on hire to the ECCC but there were others for short periods of time.

Typical traffics in which the ECCC was engaged included coal from collieries on the Erewash to the generating station at Long Eaton and a variety of destinations on the river Soar up to Leicester, cast iron pipes from Stantons and gravel to Nottingham.

Initially ECCC was controlled from an office at Friar Lane, Leicester with Wilfred Curtis as Chairman and G. H. Wood as the managing director. Curtis resigned in April 1937, being replaced by John Whittington whilst H. S. Jespersen took over as manager from

A GUCCC pair in Regent's Canal Dock being loaded from the motor vessel KEMPHAAN. The dock played a major role in securing traffic for the canal with transhipment to and from sea-going craft being a regular feature. (The Waterways Archive, Gloucester)

1 January 1939.

In 1941 the Grand Union had the opportunity to acquire most of the boats of the Warwickshire Canal Carrying Company that was based at Nuneaton. These were engaged almost exclusively on carrying coal from the Warwickshire coalfield to destinations on the Grand Union and Oxford Canals. It was decided to proceed but that the £7,500 purchase would be made by the ECCC, rather than direct by the parent company. As a result on 1 December 1941 eight pairs joined the fleet initially on hire from the Grand Union but being purchased by the ECCC in April 1942 when a new fleet numbering system was introduced, matching that for the GUCCC. This included the two Yarwoods pairs and ELIZABETH & CHARLES acquired from Edward Lane of Stowehill, near Weedon, for £550 in February 1942. All the older boats had been disposed of by now. The Warwickshire boats continued to operate completely separately from the Leicester-based craft.

500	TWEED & HARRIETT	506	PREMIER & DOROTHY
501	CALDER & WEY	507	MARGARET & THELMA
502	ENTERPRISE & RIVAL	508	ELIZABETH & CHARLES
503	JOAN & MERSEY	509	CYPRUS & CEDAR
504	ALICE & FLORENCE	510	ELM & ASH
505	KING & DAUNTLESS		

Early in 1944 the Grand Union carried out a review, which found that the cost of hiring the GUCCC boats to the ECCC was not cost effective and the practice came to an end on 1 March. Likewise owing to the heavy maintenance costs of the Warwickshire boats it was deemed uneconomic to keep them in commission and most were sold off or went into store at Stockley Dock. Such traffic as remained on the northern waters was handled directly by the GUCCC.

The Shipping Company: On 18 August 1937 the Grand Union (Stevedoring and Wharfage) Co. Ltd., a Grand Union subsidiary that operated in the Regent's Canal Dock, acquired the Dutch-built

The motor boat SOUTHALL forges across Wolverton Aqueduct on her way south with a load of road stone from Nuneaton for delivery to a wharf on West London. (The Waterways Archive, Gloucester)

A GUCCC pair, believed to be TUCANA & TAURUS, delivering their load of coal to the power station at John Dickinson's Apsley mill. Deliveries of coal to this mill were continued by the GUCCC's successors until May 1963. (Author's collection)

366-ton steam ship MERWEDE for £8,000. The boat was renamed MARSWORTH and was hired out at £560 per annum to the GUCCC to operate. At the same time two other ships were chartered and a regular service was then started to Rotterdam and Antwerp so as to attract more trade to the dock. The GUCCC's tenure was short lived as the Grand Union decided to set up a separate subsidiary to operate the ships and Grand Union (Shipping) Ltd. was incorporated on 27 November.

The company went on to establish a trans-Atlantic service to Canada and the Great Lakes and acquired two more ships – the Ayr-built 738-ton steamer KATHLEEN for £9,250 in December 1939 that was renamed BLISWORTH and the Middlesborough-built 791-ton steamer ESKWOOD in January 1944 that was renamed KILWORTH. After the war the 857-ton motor vessel KNEBWORTH was

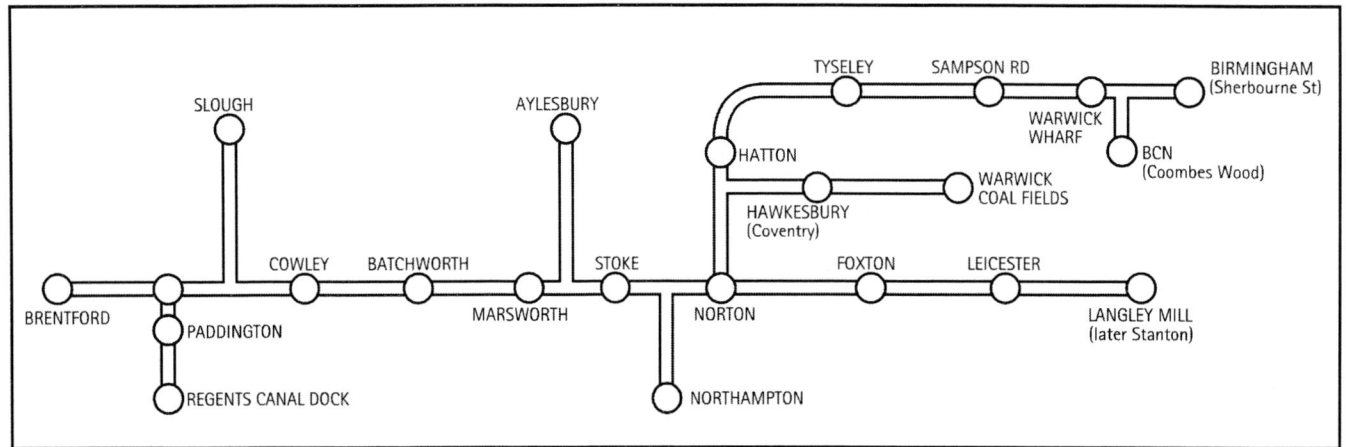

Boat Control Chart

built for the company by the Burntisland shipyard in Fife being completed in June 1946 at a cost of £53,700 and a similar ship, the 865-ton MV BOSWORTH followed from the same yard in September.

Boat Control: At an early stage the GUCCC realised that some form of control was essential for its large fleet and it instituted a unique system to check the movement of its craft. A large master chart - some 11ft long and 4ft high - was hung on one of the walls of the Bulls Bridge fleet office. The chart showed twenty-three strategic places along the 380 miles of waterway over which the fleet operated. Each of these places represented a Reporting Office from which a note was sent each morning to Bulls Bridge of all the boats that had passed on the previous day or were loading, discharging or awaiting orders.

The boats were represented on the chart by coloured discs bearing the appropriate fleet number - red for loaded, green for empty. At 9am each day the clerk in charge of boat control sorted out the reports and then began the task of "moving the boats" with the discs being transferred to their new places on the chart as indicated by the reports. The discs were always kept on the right-hand side of the route to show in which direction the craft were travelling. Not only did this system provide a quick means of reference but slow moving boats could be spotted, whilst the numbers of boats arriving at any one point could be seen and requirements at loading and discharging points assessed, with empty craft being transferred as necessary.

The GUCCC fleet colours were originally two shades of blue but in 1937, Coronation year, a patriotic livery of red, white and blue was adopted. In the war years the standard colours were maroon and blue with a simplified form of lettering being used on the cabin sides. The company was always progressive in its outlook and the improved design of the boats was a good example, the naval architect being employed for this purpose. The fleet was fitted with powerful electric headlights making travelling and lock working at night much easier. Electric lights were also fitted in the cabins whereas its biggest rival, Fellows, Morton & Clayton Ltd., used paraffin lamps throughout its history.

The company's headquarters were based at a series of different locations. Initially the offices were at Cotton End, Northampton but with the expansion premises were taken at 20 Bucklesbury, London EC4. Towards the end of 1936 there was a short-term move to Sackville House, 149 Fenchurch Street, London EC3. Then in April 1937 the company moved to the Port of London Building, Seething Lane, London EC3 near the Tower of London where the Grand Union was centralising all its operations. Meanwhile key clerical staff had been based at Bulls Bridge from the autumn of 1935.

In 1930 the Grand Union had purchased a second-hand barge to be used as a floating school for the children of the boat crews. It was converted for its new role at Walker's yard at Rickmansworth at an all-in cost to the company of £318.75 and at a ceremony at Paddington in September 1930 was named ELSDALE after the Reverend Daniel Elsdale who was particularly concerned for the welfare of the children. The barge was then towed to West Drayton where it served until 16 August 1939 when it was moved to Bulls Bridge, hoisted out onto the canal bank where it became the responsibility of the GUCCC for a nominal £1 annual rent.

The Second World War: In the war years the GUCCC fleet played an important role with waterborne goods often arriving days before goods sent by rail. An important traffic was the "Beer Run" with barrels being loaded at a north London wharf close to Arthur Guinness & Son Ltd's Park Royal brewery, destined for Birmingham where a return load of empty barrels was taken on. The round trip took about a week and nine pairs were on the traffic at one time. Normally the crew was four handed, the men being specially selected for the work, as it was an extremely tight schedule. On one

FORNAX & RA pause on their way to Birmingham to be gauged at Norton Junction, where the canal to Leicester branches off on the left. By measuring the boat's freeboard the weight of the cargo could be determined, and hence the toll payable, from tables kept at each of the toll offices. (The Waterways Archive, Gloucester)

occasion a pair did the journey from Birmingham to London in a record 37¾ hours. The Park Royal brewery was built between 1933 and 1936, the architect being Sir Giles Gilbert Scott. It closed in 2005 with production reverting to the famous St. James's Gate brewery in Dublin.

These beer boats proved highly successful despite the difficulties operating in the wartime blackout and with the overnight insertion of stop planks at key locations as a precaution against possible flooding as a result of bomb damage.

The boats helped in other ways too. In 1941 the London Fire Brigade hired five motors - ALCOR, ASTEROPE, AURIGA, CALLISTO and DORADO - at £6 per month each for fire-fighting duties in the London docks. By September 1943 no less than fifteen motors were employed in this way and a pair - GEMINI & TAURUS - was on hire to the War Department.

One of the results of the war was that the company had to vacate its offices in the Port of London Building. When the blitz started early in September 1940 virtually all operations had to be moved to Transport House, Reservoir Road, Ruislip where they remained until the end of 1950.

On the management side Ernest John Woolley, who was a colonel in the army, had to give up his position as chairman owing to his military duties but he remained as a director. The managing director, John Miller now took on the additional role of chairman being assisted by John Whittington who had joined the board in 1937, and by Cyril Saywood who was appointed as an additional director in March 1945.

The war years also saw the Grand Union tidy up the GUCCC's financial position when, in May 1945, it issued £183,599 of a new 3½% debenture stock and used £177,000 of the proceeds to take up

A GUCCC boatman taking pride in the appearance of his boats ELECTRA & ETHIOPIA by polishing their brasses whilst they were tied up at the Bulls Bridge Depot. (Author's collection)

A crowded scene at the northern end of the embankment across the Great Ouse valley at Wolverton with two pairs passing whilst a third pair is in the background a short distance below Cosgrove Lock. (The Waterways Archive, Gloucester)

shares in the subsidiary, which was then able to redeem its own debentures. At the same time £6,434 was used to make all the shares now fully paid. As a result of this the GUCCC lost its Stock Exchange listing and reverted to being a private limited company.

The Fleet reduces in size: Meanwhile the company had begun to take active steps to dispose of some of its surplus craft, particularly the early Royalty and Star Class boats. HAWK had been sold for £130 to Hubert Coles of Thrupp in March 1936 and JOSEPHINE MARGUERITE went to Edward Wood of Bedworth in August 1939 for £80. Both eventually found their way into the S. E. Barlow fleet as HAWKE and UNION JACK.

Early in 1940 negotiations were opened with Stanton & Staveley Ltd., which operated a large ironworks close to the Erewash Canal and over the next two years six pairs of surplus craft were sold for £7,100. One pair - PLEIONE & PLEIADES - had to be returned as unsatisfactory with VESTA & CANIS being supplied in their place.

Between 1941 and 1943 three pairs and a single motor were sold to A. Wander Ltd., the Ovaltine manufacturers based at Kings Langley, for £3,400. Another two pairs and a butty went to the Samuel Barlow Coal Co. Ltd. of Birmingham and Braunston for £2,940; three pairs went direct to S. E. Barlow of Tamworth; three motors and four butties to L. B. Faulkner who had been appointed as the company's Leighton Buzzard agent in April 1941, three pairs to the London Midland & Scottish Railway Company; two pairs to John Green (Carriers) Ltd. of Macclesfield; another to the River Severn Catchment Board; two butties to the Manchester Ship Canal Company and a pair to its Bridgewater Department; and several carriers purchased single boats.

The butty THOTH southbound at West Hyde on 22 August 1936. (Hertfordshire County Council)

Several boats were sold for other than carrying - in 1945 DUCHESS was bought by the Northampton Sea Cadet Corps and after the war the motors CALLISTO and HESPERUS and butties GLOSSOR and PHOSPHOROUS were sold for conversion to pleasure craft. These disposals were all of Star Class boats but in 1946 three pairs of the Town Class went to the Flixborough Shipping Co. of Horninglow for £2,727.

Meanwhile several boats became maintenance craft, particularly the Middle Northwich Class that, with their "Vee" bottoms, were somewhat unstable when loaded and hence tended to be unpopular with the boatmen. However they made ideal ice-breaking craft - several motors including SICKLE, THEOPHILUS and TYCHO were converted for this purpose. All the Middle Northwich butties except TAURUS were sold to the Grand Union for £3,000 for adaption for either pumping or dredging work and in 1945 this company paid £4,181 for another eleven motors, including five of the Royalty Class, and three butties for maintenance duties. Four Royalty butties went to Thomas Clayton (Paddington) Ltd., another Grand Union subsidiary company, in 1943 for conversion to hulks for carrying rubbish from the London Boroughs of Marylebone and Paddington.

On 1 January 1948 the Grand Union Canal Company and its various subsidiaries were nationalised and by this time the GUCCC fleet had been whittled down to 126 motors and 130 butties. SPEEDY was the only ACC motor left and FOMALHAUT the only Little

Ricky motor. Three ACC butties survived, COUNTESS, PRINCESS and RUGBY, but only MARS of the prototype Star Class and GLAXY of the Little Ricky Class. Meanwhile the Town Class was intact except for the three pairs sold to Flixborough Shipping, the motor RENTON which had become a maintenance boat and BARRHEAD, GLOSSOR and LAMBOURNE which had been sold.

Nationalisation: Soon after nationalisation the British Transport Commission purchased the carrying business of GUCCC rivals Fellows, Morton & Clayton and one hundred and ten boats joined the fleet based at Bulls Bridge, both now trading under the name of British Waterways.

As traffics were continuing to be lost the surplus of craft persisted and steps were taken to re-allocate them. In 1949 twelve motorboats were transferred to the South Western Division, based on Gloucester where they became maintenance craft being numbered from B1 to B12. In the same year another three motors went to the North Western Division's maintenance fleet based on Northwich.

This move continued into the 1950s and 1960s until former Grand Union craft were appearing on maintenance work across the nationalised canal system. For instance in 1958 OAKLEY, PADDINGTON and SOUTHALL were transferred to the North Eastern Division and in 1962 they were joined by FENNY and NABURN whilst butties ANDROMEDA, CORONIS, DIPPER and DUBHE were all working on the river Trent.

Other craft undertook a very different role. In the winter of 1949 THEMIS was converted to a passenger carrying trip boat and DENEBOLA soon joined her. They operated public and private trips in the London area and from Uxbridge and Watford. In 1958 they

AYNHO & AYR, one of the Harland & Wolff "Town Class" pairs, are forced to use one of original narrow locks at Stockton on their way to Birmingham, as the new wide one was undergoing repair work. There used to be several lime and cement works in this area and the remains of one is just beyond the lock. (The Waterways Archive, Gloucester)

Children from narrow boat families with their teacher Mrs Oakley on board the school barge ELSDALE at Bulls Bridge. The school was established in September 1930, the barge being converted at Walker Brothers boatyard at Rickmansworth and was based at West Drayton. Later she sprang a leak and ended up on the bank at Bulls Bridge where she remained in service until 1960. (Hugh McKnight Collection)

were renamed WATER KELPIE and WATER FAIRY. In May 1957 British Waterways introduced the luxury boat WATER RAMBLER (ex STAR), which operated week-long cruises with the guests staying in convenient hotels overnight. She introduced the practice of naming the trip boats with the "water" series of names. And in the same month WATER SPRITE (ex PISCES) began operating trips on the Worcester & Birmingham Canal based at Tardebigge.

In May 1959 British Waterways launched their Zoo Water Bus service that operated from Little Venice to London's Zoo in Regent's Park. PERSEUS was converted for this role and renamed WATER BUCK and WATER WAGTAIL (ex COROLLA) and WATER OUZEL (ex SUN) joined her in 1960 whilst WATER NYMPH (ex SOUTHERN CROSS) also operated on the service.

British Waterways also entered the hire industry and other boats were converted for this purpose. Examples were the fore end of ANTONY becoming the hire boat WATER LILAC, of ANTLIA becoming WATER VIXEN and of ENCELADUS becoming WATER VALIANT. Meanwhile the stern ends of AURORA and INDUS became WATER VIOLET and WATER REED and there was a series of others.

Many of the craft saw further carrying service with new owners, one of the best known being the Willow Wren Canal Carrying Company Limited, which was formed at the end of 1953 to try and revive canal traffics. It went on to purchase twenty-two former GUCCC boats together with fourteen from the former FMC fleet.

When the newly-formed British Waterways Board decided to give up all but two of its carrying contracts in the south-east, a new Willow Wren company was formed, hiring many of the now redundant boats and succeeding in retaining some of the contracts for a while. Willow Wren finally gave up in 1970 with the hired boats reverting to British Waterways but even then several were sold on to other carrying concerns.

Another pioneer was the Birmingham & Midland Canal Carrying Company Limited that was formed in March 1965 and acquired several GUCCC craft. Blue Line Canal Carriers Limited of Braunston, which only gave up carrying in 1970 due to the closure of the factory it served at Southall, was another. And as late as 1980 the Threefellows Canal Carrying Company was operating BUXTON & ABOYNE, CHISWICK & TAURUS, HALSALL & BANBURY and WHITBY & PICTOR carrying aggregates on the river Soar near Leicester and other boats joined them before the traffic finished in the 1990s.

And sadly several boats were scrapped. For example the motor SPEEDY saw no service with British Waterways and was lying sunk at Stockley Dock in 1948 whilst the wooden butties GLAXY and PLEIADES were hauled out onto the bank and burnt at Cowley in 1961. And in 1958 a series of boats, involving several of the Royalty Class butties were deliberately sunk in a gravel pit at Harefield in an exercise described by the Inland Waterways Association as the "Modern Scapa Flow".

More positive were a series of sales to private owners starting as early as April 1948 when the disused butty PRINCESS was sold to J. Goddard for £100, and many others followed over the years. Today many of the former GUCCC craft are still around the system, lovingly cared for by their private owners with some still being used for carrying when cargoes become available and some being painted up in the various GUCCC liveries to serve as a reminder of the once great Grand Union Fleet.

A regular GUCCC traffic was grain, imported through the London Docks, barged up the Thames to Brentford where it was transhipped to narrow boats and much was delivered to Whitworth's Mill on the river Nene at Wellingborough as shown here. Traffic to the mill was continued by the GUCCC's successors until April 1969. (Robert Wilson Collection)

GRAND UNION CANAL CARRYING CO. LTD MOTOR BOATS

No	Name	Builder/Date	Registered	Gauged	Pair	Fate
1	ACHERNAR	N 30.10.35	Br 546 09.11.35	12431 21.11.35	203	DIWE
2	ADVANCE	A 12.11.30	Dv 417 02.12.30	11888 18.01.15	338	scrapped
3	ALDEBARAN	H 02.01.35	Dv 462 19.02.35	12359 12.02.35	322	6/43 SBC
4	ALCOR	N 01.11.35	Br 550 09.11.35	12550 29.06.36	208	DIWE
5	ALGOL	N 08.11.35	Br 554 18.12.35	12433 22.11.35	215	6/40 S&S
6	ANTONY	N 08.11.35	Br 552 18.12.35	12474 13.03.36	255	DIWE
7	ANTARES	I 05.03.35	Rk 33 19.03.35	12371 12.03.35	361	7/42 TGC
8	ANTLIA	L 22.01.36	B 1592 19.06.36	12463 10.03.36	304	DIWE
9	AQUARIUS	N 16.11.35	Br 556 18.12.35	12491 27.03.36	210	DIWE
10	AQUILA	K 21.06.35	Br 490 26.06.35	12440 26.11.35	213	DIWE
11	ARCAS	N 16.11.35	Br 558 18.12.35	12582 20.10.36	221	DIWE
12	ARCHIMEDES	N 23.11.35	Br 560 18.12.35	12446 28.11.35	308	11/45 GUC
13	ARCTURUS	I 24.10.34	Rk 28 20.11.34	12356 11.02.35	358	8/42 AWL
14	ARIES	M 06.07.35	Rk 40 16.07.35	12540 22.06.36	217	1/44 LMS
15	ASTEROPE	N 23.11.35	Br 562 18.12.35	12466 10.03.36	202	DIWE
16	ATLAS	N 29.11.35	Br 565 18.12.35	12529 18.06.36	220	DIWE
17	AURIGA	K 14.06.35	Br 512 03.09.35	12478 23.03.36	214	DIWE
18	BARGUS	N 29.11.35	Br 567 18.12.35	12487 25.03.36	235	DIWE
19	BELLATRIX	L 30.10.35	Never registered	12429 21.11.35	305	7/42 sold
20	BOOTES	N 06.12.35	Br 569 18.12.35	12542 23.06.36	232	DIWE
21	CALLISTO	N 06.12.35	Br 571 18.12.35	12548 26.06.36	247	4/47 sold
22	CAPRICORN	K 10.07.35	Br 504 24.07.35	12420 18.11.35	264	DIWE
23	CASSIOPEIA	K 29.06.35	Br 494 24.07.35	12525 17.06.36	265	DIWE
24	CASTOR	M 27.04.35	Rk 36 21.05.35	12520 15.06.36	335	4/47 LBF
25	CENTAURI	K 12.06.35	Br 500 24.07.35	12383 08.10.35	250	DIWE
26	CEPHEUS	K 21.06.35	Br 488 26.06.35	12389 10.10.35	266	11/45 GUC
27	CERES	K 03.09.35	Br 532 25.09.35	12427 20.11.35	326	9/47 MSC
28	CLYPEUS	L 06.06.35	Br 498 24.07.35	12423 19.11.35	260	DIWE
29	COLUMBA	N 16.12.35	Br 573 18.12.35	12476 16.03.36	269	4/47 HDE
30	COMET	K 17.08.35	Br 524 03.09.35	12385 09.10.35	313	DIWE
31	COROLLA	N 16.12.35	Br 575 18.12.35	12494 27.03.36	246	DIWE
32	CORONA	N 16.12.35	Br 577 18.12.35	12552 30.06.36	259	11/45 GUC
33	DEIMOS	N 20.12.35	Br 580 22.01.36	12489 26.03.36	268	DIWE
34	DELPHINUS	L 19.09.35	B 1578 18.10.35	12506 09.06.36	271	6/42 TGC
35	DENEBOLA	N 20.12.35	Br 582 22.01.36	12501 08.06.36	272	DIWE
36	DORADO	N 20.12.35	Br 584 22.01.36	12461 07.03.36	344	DIWE
37	DORNEY COURT	A 07.01.35	Dv 405 25.03.30*	11956 05.06.30	276	6/41 SEB
38	DUKE	C 16.10.31	Tr 117 01.12.31	12338 14.10.32	273	11/45 GUC
39	EDWARD	C 30.11.31	Dv 429 22.03.32	12315 15.04.32	206	11/45 GUC
40	ELECTRA	P 23.10.35	Rk 48 05.11.35	12546 25.06.36	278	8/41 S&S
41	ENCELADUS	L 21.08.35	B 1577 20.09.35	12391 10.10.35	306	DIWE
42	ERIDANUS	L 22.07.35	Br 534 25.09.35	12452 04.03.36	300	DIWE
43	FOMALHAUT	P 23.11.25	Rk 50 05.11.35	12469 12.03.36	291	DIWE
44	FORNAX	P 06.12.35	Rk 52 08.01.36	12504 09.06.36	341	11/45 TSE
45	GEMINI	K 29.07.35	Br 516 03.09.35	12444 27.11.35	216	DIWE
46	GEORGE	B 02.02.29	Tr 108 05.02.29	12180 12.03.29	388	4/36 GUC
47	GRUS	P 29.01.36	Rk 54 08.01.36	12537 22.06.36	282	2/41 AWL
48	THE HAWK	A 29.01.29	Dv 398 18.06.29	X5614 29.02.28	347	3/36 sold
49	HENRY	D 15.07.31	Rk 22 08.10.31	12310 12.04.32	212	11/45 GUC
50	HERCULES	K 21.09.35	Br 540 25.09.35	12438 26.11.35	384	6/46 LMS
51	HESPERUS	P 13.02.36	Rk 57 18.02.36	12516 13.06.36	331	7/47 sold
52	HYDRA	K 08.07.35	Br 496 24.07.35	12538 22.06.36	293	DIWE
53	HYPERION	K 15.05.35	Br 514 03.09.35	12448 28.11.35	292	11/47 SEB
54	ISIS	P 13.02.36	Rk 60 18.02.36	12480 23.03.36	290	1/41 AWL
55	JOSEPHINE M'	A 22.10.32	Dv 436 01.11.32	X5612 08.12.27	258	8/39 sold
56	JUPITER	J 04.12.34	Br 487 19.12.34	12362 07.03.35	310	5/42 JGC
57	LACERTA	L 04.07.35	Br 520 03.09.35	12553 24.08.36	302	DIWE
58	LIBRA	L 16.10.35	Br 548 09.11.35	12425 19.11.35	249	4/47 sold
59	MAIA	P 10.03.36	Rk 62 21.04.36	12559 25.08.36	311	3/41 S&S
60	MERCURY	K 13.09.35	Br 536 25.09.35	12404 18.10.35	219	11/45 GUC
61	MEROPE	P 09.04.36	Rk 64 21.04.36	12617 16.11.36	312	11/41 S&S
62	MIMAS	M 12.09.35	Rk 46 17.09.35	12442 27.11.35	316	9/43 AWL
63	MIRA	P 16.05.36	Rk 66 21.04.36	12522 16.06.36	314	5/41 S&S
64	MIZAR	P 16.05.36	Rk 68 19.05.36	12510 10.06.36	387	7/47 SEB
65	MONOCEROS	P 25.05.36	Rk 70 19.05.36	12594 27.10.36	309	6/47 LBF
66	NEPTUNE	I 18.12.34	Rk 30 18.12.34	12381 28.03.35	209	4/43 SBC
67	OBERON	M 02.08.35	Rk 42 30.07.35	Never gauged	321	6/43 LMS
68	ORPHEUS	P 04.06.36	Rk 72 16.06.36	12561 25.08.36	329	6/47 LBF
69	PEGASUS	K 10.07.35	Br 502 24.07.35	12406 19.10.35	327	DIWE
70	PERSEUS	K 17.07.35	Br 506 24.07.35	12450 29.11.35	332	DIWE
71	PHOBOS	K 23.07.35	Br 508 03.09.35	12387 09.10.35	294	DIWE
72	PHOENIX	M 14.06.35	Rk 38 18.06.35	12416 25.10.35	330	9/42 JGC
73	PISCES	L 11.05.35	B 1574 20.09.35	12454 05.03.36	339	DIWE
74	PLANET	K 04.10.35	Br 544 23.10.35	12413 24.10.35	317	11/45 GUC
75	PLATO	K 21.08.35	Br 528 03.09.35	12485 25.03.36	380	2/41 sold
76	PLEIONE	Q 06.12.35	Br 564 18.12.35	12544 23.06.36	333	DIWE
77	PRAESEPE	Q 12.01.36	Br 579 22.01.36	12545 24.06.36	328	4/41 TSE
78	PRINCE	D 15.07.31	Rk 23 08.10.31	12313 14.04.32	337	11/45 GUC
79	RADIANT	O 14.11.35	B 1591 19.06.36	12482 24.03.36	343	DIWE
80	SAGITTA	L 20.06.35	Br 526 03.09.35	12395 11.10.35	355	DIWE
81	SCORPIO	L 04.10.35	Cv 534 31.12.36	12411 24.10.35	307	DIWE
82	SCULPTOR	L 29.11.35	B 1584 15.05.36	12499 06.06.36	377	DIWE

No	Name	Builder/Date	Registered	Gauged	Pair	Fate	No	Name	Builder/Date	Registered	Gauged	Pair	Fate
83	SEXTANS	O 07.01.36	Never registered	12496 28.03.36	353	1942 MOWT	126	BUXTON	S 28.07.36	Cv 540 25.02.37	12608 05.11.36	245	DIWE
84	SICKLE	O 17.03.36	Rk 187 21.09.37	12534 20.06.36	350	1942 MOWT	127	CALDY	S 08.08.36	Rk 92 22.09.36	12557 25.08.36	248	DIWE
85	SOUTHERN X	K 08.08.35	Br 518 03.09.35	12409 23.10.35	334	DIWE	128	CALSTOCK	S 29.12.36	Br 624 27.01.37	12736 16.02.38	251	DIWE
86	SPEEDY	A 15.02.34	Tr 120 06.03.34	11781 29.01.14	356	DIWE	129	CAMBOURNE	S 29.12.36	Br 625 27.01.37	12698 05.03.37	252	DIWE
87	STAR	K 26.09.35	Br 542 23.10.35	12459 06.03.36	351	DIWE	130	CHERTSEY	S 29.01.37	Cv 539 25.02.37	12694 04.03.37	253	DIWE
88	SUN	K 14.08.35	Br 522 03.09.35	12418 26.10.35	315	DIWE	131	CHISWICK	S 29.01.37	Rk 151 20.04.37	12659 12.02.37	254	DIWE
89	TAYGETA	O 02.04.36	B 1587 19.06.36	12527 17.06.36	378	DIWE	132	COLESHILL	S 29.01.37	Cv 547 02.09.37	12663 13.02.37	256	DIWE
90	THEMIS	K 18.05.35	Br 510 03.09.35	12393 11.10.35	375	DIWE	133	CANTLEY	S 29.01.37	Rk 166 20.07.37	12669 16.02.37	257	DIWE
91	THEOPHILUS	O 19.04.36	B 1598 17.07.36	12606 05.11.36	372	1942 MOWT	134	CARNABY	S 29.01.37	Cv 542 25.02.37	Never gauged 261		DIWE
92	TUCANA	O 07.05.36	B 1595 19.06.36	12518 15.06.36	370	DIWE	135	DARLEY	S 29.01.37	Rk 160 15.06.37	12661 12.02.37	267	DIWE
93	TYCHO	O 14.05.36	B 1601 18.12.36	12503 08.06.36	373	1942 MOWT	136	DOVER	S 26.02.37	Rk 184 21.09.37	12715 18.03.37	270	DIWE
94	UMBRIEL	M 21.08.35	Rk 44 17.09.35	12407 23.10.35	381	9/41 TSE	137	DUNSTABLE	S 26.02.37	Rk 154 18.05.37	12713 17.03.37	274	9/46 FSC
95	VENUS	H 25.11.34	Tr 124 01.01.35	12375 26.03.35	352	9/43 RSCB	138	EDGWARE	S 26.02.37	Rk 172 20.07.37	12710 13.03.37	275	DIWE
96	VESTA	K 29.08.35	Br 530 03.09.35	12472 13.03.36	295	11/41 S&S	139	ELSTREE	S 26.02.37	Rk 161 15.06.37	12708 12.03.37	277	DIWE
97	VICTORIA	C 16.10.31	Br 481 11.11.31	12331 11.10.32	205	11/45 GUC	140	EPSOM	S 24.03.37	Rk 194 18.01.38	12764 23.03.38	279	9/46 FSC
98	VIRGO	K 04.07.35	Br 493 24.07.35	12397 12.10.35	383	DIWE	141	FENNY	S 24.03.37	Rk 192 16.11.37	12770 05.04.38	280	DIWE
99	WILLIAM	C 30.11.31	Rk 26 21.04.32	12323 21.04.32	204	11/47 sold	142	FULBOURNE	S 24.03.37	Rk 174 20.07.37	12740 21.02.38	281	DIWE
100	ZODIAC	O 04.06.36	Rk 140 16.03.37	12592 24.10.36	301	DIWE	143	GAINSBOROUGHS 24.03.37		Rk 177 21.09.37	12744 03.03.38	283	DIWE
101	ABER	R 16.07.36	Cv 543 29.04.37	12572 28.08.36	207	DIWE	144	GREENOCK	S 23.04.37	Rk 167 20.07.37	12758 17.03.38	284	DIWE
102	ALTON	R 28.07.36	Cv 537 28.01.37	12612 06.11.36	201	DIWE	145	GREENLAW	S 14.03.37	Rk 157 15.06.37	12738 21.02.38	285	DIWE
103	ALDGATE	R 08.08.36	Rk 133 16.02.37	12555 24.08.36	211	DIWE	146	HAMPSTEAD	S 05.04.37	Rk 163 15.06.37	12757 17.03.38	286	DIWE
104	ASCOT	R 18.08.36	Cv 545 03.06.37	12577 19.10.36	218	DIWE	147	HADLEY	S 19.05.37	Rk 171 20.07.37	12734 16.02.38	287	DIWE
105	AYNHO	R 18.08.36	Br 609 09.12.36	12601 29.10.36	222	DIWE	148	HAWKESBURY	S 19.05.37	Rk 170 20.07.37	12732 15.02.38	288	DIWE
106	BALDOCK	R 27.08.36	Cv 532 31.12.36	12604 04.11.36	226	DIWE	149	HALSALL	T 30.06.36	Rk 79 21.07.36	12566 26.08.36	289	DIWE
107	BANSTEAD	R 27.08.36	Br 605 09.12.36	12766 24.03.38	225	DIWE	150	KENILWORTH	T 30.06.36	Rk 80 21.07.36	12627 21.11.36	296	DIWE
108	BADSEY	R 08.09.36	Br 619 27.01.37	12674 19.02.37	227	DIWE	151	KELSO	T 10.07.36	Rk 84 11.08.36	12629 23.11.36	297	DIWE
109	BARNET	R 08.09.36	Br 101 21.09.27	12625 20.11.36	228	DIWE	152	LADYRANK	T 10.07.36	Rk 85 11.08.36	12639 30.11.36	298	DIWE
110	BAINTON	R 18.09.36	Br 588 09.12.36	12587 22.10.36	234	DIWE	153	LETCHWORTH	T 22.07.36	Rk 89 11.08.36	12590 23.10.36	303	DIWE
111	BATH	R 18.09.36	Br 590 28.10.36	12750 14.03.38	229	9/46 FSC	154	LANCING	T 22.07.36	Rk 88 11.08.36	12574 28.08.36	299	DIWE
112	BATTERSEA	R 02.10.36	Br 592 28.10.36	12642 30.11.36	230	DIWE	155	NABURN	T 08.08.36	Rk 175 20.07.37	12568 27.08.36	319	DIWE
113	BEAULIEU	R 02.10.36	Rk 114 15.12.36	12665 15.02.37	231	DIWE	156	NUNEATON	T 08.08.36	Rk 155 15.06.37	12563 26.08.36	320	DIWE
114	BARNHAM	R 15.10.36	Br 594 28.10.36	12637 27.11.36	233	DIWE	157	NUTFIELD	T 18.08.36	Rk 97 22.09.36	12580 20.10.36	318	DIWE
115	BELFAST	R 15.10.36	Br 607 09.12.36	12584 21.10.36	223	DIWE	158	OTLEY	T 18.08.36	Rk 96 22.09.36	12621 18.11.36	323	DIWE
116	BEXHILL	R 15.10.36	Br 596 28.10.36	12610 06.11.36	236	DIWE	159	OAKLEY	T 22.08.36	Rk 98 20.10.36	12631 24.11.36	324	DIWE
117	BICESTER	R 30.10.36	Br 602 09.12.36	12702 08.03.37	237	DIWE	160	PADDINGTON	T 04.09.36	Rk 99 20.10.36	12596 27.10.36	325	DIWE
118	BILSTER	R 30.10.36	Br 600 09.12.36	12679 22.02.37	238	11/45 GUC	161	PINNER	T 04.09.36	Br 598 09.12.36	12589 23.10.36	336	DIWE
119	BLETCHLEY	R 17.11.36	Br 613 09.12.36	12644 01.12.36	224	DIWE	162	PURTON	T 10.09.36	Rk 104 20.10.36	12614 07.11.36	340	DIWE
120	BOGNOR	R 17.11.36	Br 611 09.12.36	12683 24.02.37	239	DIWE	163	READING	T 07.10.36	Rk 111 15.12.36	12599 28.10.36	342	DIWE
121	BIRMINGHAM	R 17.11.36	Br 615 09.12.36	12672 17.02.37	240	DIWE	164	RENTON	T 07.10.36	Rk 118 15.12.36	12633 26.11.36	345	1942 MOWT
122	BOURNEMOUTH	R 12.12.36	Br 622 27.01.37	12657 11.02.37	241	DIWE	165	RENFREW	T 13.10.36	Rk 113 15.12.36	12623 20.11.36	346	DIWE
123	BRISTOL	R 12.12.36	Br 623 27.01.37	12655 11.02.37	242	DIWE	166	RUFFORD	T 13.10.36	Br 606 09.12.36	12619 16.11.36	348	DIWE
124	BUCKDEN	R 12.12.36	Br 621 27.01.37	12652 10.02.37	243	DIWE	167	SALTAIRE	T 24.10.36	Rk 122 15.12.36	12696 05.03.37	349	DIWE
125	BARROW	S 16.07.36	Rk 86 11.08.36	12570 27.08.36	244	DIWE	168	SEAFORD	T 24.10.36	Rk 135 16.02.37	12726 11.02.38	354	DIWE

No	Name	Builder/Date	Registered	Gauged	Pair	Fate	No	Name	Builder/Date	Registered	Gauged	Pair	Fate
169	SHIRLEY	T 29.10.36	Rk 121 15.12.36	12646 02.12.36	357	DIWE	178	TADWORTH	T 12.01.37	Rk 136 16.02.37	12711 17.03.37	368	DIWE
170	SLOUGH	T 29.10.36	Rk 119 15.12.36	12635 27.11.36	359	DIWE	179	THAXTED	T 15.01.37	Rk 164 20.07.37	12671 17.02.37	374	DIWE
171	SOUTHALL	T 21.11.36	Rk 130 19.01.37	12685 24.02.37	360	DIWE	180	TIPTON	T 15.01.37	Rk 185 21.09.37	12677 22.02.37	376	DIWE
172	STAMFORD	T 19.11.36	Rk 176 20.07.37	12724 10.02.38	362	DIWE	181	TOWCESTER	T 15.02.37	Rk 144 20.04.37	12709 13.03.37	371	DIWE
173	STANTON	T 19.11.36	Cv 536 31.12.36	12668 16.02.37	363	DIWE	182	TARPORLEY	T 15.02.37	Rk 147 20.04.37	12703 09.03.37	369	DIWE
174	STIRLING	T 21.11.36	Rk 126 19.01.37	12650 09.02.37	364	DIWE	183	TYSELEY	T 08.03.37	Rk 149 20.04.37	12741 09.03.38	379	DIWE
175	STRATFORD	T 15.12.36	Rk 128 19.01.37	12692 03.03.37	365	DIWE	184	USWORTH	T 08.03.37	Rk 178 21.09.37	12751 15.03.38	382	DIWE
176	SUDBURY	T 15.12.36	Rk 129 19.01.37	12729 12.02.38	366	DIWE	185	WHITBY	T 23.04.37	Rk 195 18.01.38	Never gauged	385	DIWE
177	SUTTON	T 15.12.36	Rk 182 21.09.37	12681 23.02.37	367	DIWE	186	YEOFORD	T 23.04.37	Cv 546 01.07.37	12760 18.03.38	386	DIWE

GRAND UNION CANAL CARRYING CO. LTD. BUTTY BOATS

No	Name	Builder/Date	Registered	Gauged	Pair	Fate	No	Name	Builder/Date	Registered	Gauged	Pair	Fate
201	ABOYNE	R 28.07.36	Cv 541 25.02.37	12609 05.11.36	102	DIWE	232	BELLEROPHON	N 06.12.35	Br 570 18.12.35	12543 23.06.36	20	DIWE
202	ACHILLLES	N 23.11.35	Br 563 18.12.35	12467 10.03.36	15	DIWE	233	BELMONT	R 15.10.36	Br 595 28.10.36	12638 28.11.36	114	DIWE
203	ACTIS	N 30.10.35	Br 547 09.11.35	12432 21.11.35	1	DIWE	234	BERKHAMSTEAD	R 18.09.36	Br 589 09.12.36	12588 22.10.36	110	DIWE
204	ADELAIDE	F 25.07.31	Rk 21 30.07.31	12324 21.04.32	99	9/43 TCP	235	BETELGEUSE	N 29.11.35	Br 568 18.12.35	12488 25.03.36	18	DIWE
205	ALBERT	E 23.11.31	Tr 116 01.12.31	12332 11.10.32	97	9/43 TCP	236	BEVERLEY	R 15.10.36	Br 597 28.10.36	12611 06.11.36	116	DIWE
206	ALEXANDRA	G 20.10.31	Br 480 11.11.31	12316 15.04.32	39	9/43 TCP	237	BIDEFORD	R 30.10.36	Br 603 09.12.36	12735 16.02.38	117	DIWE
207	ALPERTON	R 16.07.36	Cv 544 29.04.37	12573 28.08.36	101	DIWE	238	BINGLEY	R 30.10.36	Br 601 09.12.36	12680 23.02.37	118	DIWE
208	ALPHONS	N 01.11.35	Br 551 09.11.35	12551 29.06.36	4	DIWE	239	BODMIN	R 17.11.36	Br 614 09.12.36	12658 11.02.37	120	DIWE
209	ALTAIR	I 18.12.34	Rk 31 18.12.34	12382 28.03.35	66	9/46 sold	240	BORDESLEY	R 17.11.36	Br 616 09.12.36	12673 17.02.37	121	DIWE
210	ANDROMEDA	N 16.11.35	Br 557 18.12.35	12492 27.03.36	9	DIWE	241	BRANKSOME	R 17.11.36	Br 612 09.12.36	12684 24.02.37	122	DIWE
211	ANGEL	R 28.07.36	Cv 538 28.01.37	12613 06.11.36	103	DIWE	242	BRIGHTON	R 27.11.36	Br 618 09.12.36	12656 11.02.37	123	DIWE
212	ANNE	F 25.07.31	Rk 20 30.07.31	12311 13.04.32	49	9/43 TCP	243	BUDE	R 27.11.36	Br 617 09.12.36	12653 11.02.37	124	DIWE
213	ARA	K 21.06.35	Br 491 26.06.35	12441 27.11.35	10	DIWE	244	BURY	U 20.07.36	Rk 76 21.07.36	12571 27.08.36	125	DIWE
214	ARGO	K 14.06.35	Br 513 03.09.35	12479 23.03.36	17	DIWE	245	BYFIELD	U 30.07.36	Rk 87 11.08.36	12578 19.10.36	126	DIWE
215	ARGON	N 08.11.35	Br 555 18.12.35	12434 22.11.35	5	DIWE	246	CANIS	N 16.12.35	Br 576 18.12.35	12495 28.03.36	31	11/41 S&S
216	ARGUS	K 29.07.35	Br 517 03.09.35	12445 27.11.35	45	DIWE	247	CAPELLA	N 06.12.35	Br 572 18.12.35	12549 26.06.36	21	DIWE
217	ARIEL	M 06.07.35	Rk 41 16.07.35	12541 23.06.36	14	11/45 LBF	248	CARDIFF	U 18.08.36	Rk 91 22.09.36	12558 25.08.36	127	DIWE
218	ASTON	R 08.08.36	Rk 134 16.02.37	12556 24.08.36	104	DIWE	249	CARINA	L 16.10.35	Br 549 09.11.35	12426 19.11.35	58	DIWE
219	ASTRAEA	K 13.09.35	Br 537 25.09.35	12405 18.10.35	60	DIWE	250	CETUS	K 12.06.35	Br 501 24.07.35	12384 08.10.35	25	11/47 SEB
220	ATALANTA	N 29.11.35	Br 566 18.12.35	12530 18.06.36	16	6/40 S&S	251	CHALFONT	U 22.04.37	Rk 150 18.05.37	12752 15.03.38	128	DIWE
221	AURORA	N 16.11.35	Br 559 18.12.35	12583 20.10.36	11	DIWE	252	CHEAM	U 06.05.37	Rk 152 18.05.37	12733 15.02.38	129	DIWE
222	AYR	R 08.08.36	Br 610 09.12.36	12602 29.10.36	105	DIWE	253	CHESHAM	U 10.05.37	Rk 153 18.05.37	Never gauged	130	DIWE
223	BAILDON	R 15.10.36	Br 608 09.12.36	12585 21.10.36	115	DIWE	254	CHIPSTEAD	U 18.05.37	Rk 156 15.06.37	Never gauged	131	9/46 FSC
224	BAKEWELL	R 30.10.36	Br 599 09.12.36	12645 01.12.36	119	DIWE	255	CLEOPATRA	N 08.11.35	Br 553 18.12.35	12475 13.03.36	6	DIWE
225	BALHAM	R 27.08.36	Br 604 09.12.36	12767 24.03.38	107	DIWE	256	COBHAM	U 29.05.37	Rk 158 15.06.37	12756 17.03.38	132	DIWE
226	BANBURY	R 27.08.36	Cv 533 31.12.36	12605 04.11.36	106	DIWE	257	CONISTON	U 05.06.37	Rk 159 15.06.37	Never gauged	133	9/46 FSC
227	BARNES	R 08.09.36	Br 620 27.01.37	12755 16.03.38	108	DIWE	258	COOMBE ABBEY	A 22.10.32	Dv 435 01.11.32	X5599 27.06.27	55	11/41 SEB
228	BARRHEAD	R 08.09.36	Rk 180 21.09.37	12626 20.11.36	109	11/47 sold	259	CORONIS	N 16.12.35	Br 578 18.12.35	12508 10.06.36	32	DIWE
229	BAWTRY	R 18.09.36	Br 591 28.10.36	12664 13.02.37	111	DIWE	260	CORVUS	L 06.06.35	Br 499 24.07.35	12424 19.11.35	28	11/45 GUC
230	BAYSWATER	R 02.10.36	Br 593 28.10.36	12643 01.12.36	112	DIWE	261	COUGHTON	U 28.06.37	Rk 168 20.07.37	12761 18.03.38	134	DIWE
231	BEDWORTH	R 02.10.36	Rk 115 15.12.36	12666 15.02.37	113	DIWE	262	COUNT	A 15.02.34	Tr 121 06.03.34	12346 17.04.34	263	5/44 sold

No	Name	Builder/Date	Registered	Gauged	Pair	Fate	No	Name	Builder/Date	Registered	Gauged	Pair	Fate
263	COUNTESS	A 15.02.34	Tr 122 06.03.34	12347 17.04.34	262	DIWE	306	LYRA	L 21.08.35	B 1576 20.09.35	12392 10.10.35	41	DIWE
264	CRATER	K 10.07.35	Br 505 24.07.35	12421 18.11.35	22	DIWE	307	MALUS	L 04.10.35	Cv 535 31.12.36	12412 24.10.35	81	DIWE
265	CRUX	K 29.06.35	Br 495 24.07.35	12526 17.06.36	23	DIWE	308	MARCELLUS	N 23.11.35	Br 561 18.12.35	12447 28.11.35	12	DIWE
266	CYGNUS	K 21.06.35	Br 489 26.06.35	12390 10.10.35	26	DIWE	309	MARFAK	P 25.05.36	Rk 71 19.05.36	12595 27.10.36	65	8/41 S&S
267	DENTON	U 12.06.37	Rk 169 20.07.37	12728 11.02.38	135	DIWE	310	MARS	J 04.12.34	Br 486 19.12.34	12363 07.03.35	56	DIWE
268	DIPPER	N 20.12.35	Br 581 22.01.36	12484 24.03.36	33	DIWE	311	MEDUSA	P 10.03.36	Rk 63 21.04.36	12560 25.08.36	59	7/47 SEB
269	DODONA	N 16.12.35	Br 574 18.12.35	12477 16.03.36	29	DIWE	312	MERAK	P 09.04.36	Rk 65 21.04.36	12618 16.11.36	61	9/43 RSCB
270	DOWNHAM	U 29.07.37	Rk 173 20.07.37	12722 10.02.38	136	DIWE	313	METEOR	K 17.08.35	Br 525 03.09.35	12386 09.10.35	30	DIWE
271	DRACO	L 19.09.35	B 1579 18.10.35	12507 09.06.36	34	DIWE	314	MILKY WAY	P 16.05.36	Rk 67 21.04.36	12523 16.06.36	63	5/45 LBF
272	DUBHE	N 20.12.35	Br 583 22.01.36	12462 07.03.36	35	DIWE	315	MOON	K 14.08.35	Br 523 03.09.35	12419 26.10.35	88	DIWE
273	DUCHESS	G 16.06.31	Br 479 24.06.31	12339 15.10.32	38	7/45 sold	316	MUSCA	M 12.09.35	Rk 47 17.09.35	12443 27.11.35	62	9/43 LBF
274	DUDLEY	U 06.08.37	Rk 179 21.09.37	12743 09.03.38	137	DIWE	317	NEBULAE	K 04.10.35	Br 545 23.10.35	12414 24.10.35	74	6/46 LMS
275	EALING	U 18.09.37	Rk 183 21.09.37	12725 11.02.38	138	DIWE	318	NESTON	U 29.08.36	Rk 93 22.09.36	12581 20.10.36	157	DIWE
276	ELSIE EDITH	A 07.01.35	Tm 104 19.09.31*	X5439 25.09.08	37	scrapped	319	NORTON	U 12.08.36	Rk 83 11.08.36	12569 27.08.36	155	DIWE
277	ELTON	U 04.12.37	Rk 186 21.09.37	12731 11.02.38	139	DIWE	320	NUNHEAD	U 12.08.36	Rk 90 11.08.36	12564 26.08.36	156	DIWE
278	ETHIOPIA	P 23.10.35	Rk 49 05.11.35	12547 25.06.36	40	11/45 SBC	321	OCTANS	M 02.08.35	Rk 43 30.07.35	Never gauged	67	4/43 SBC
279	EWELL	U 04.12.37	Rk 189 19.10.37	12771 05.04.38	140	DIWE	322	ORION	H 02.01.35	Dv 463 19.02.35	12360 13.02.35	3	5/41 S&S
280	FELTHAM	U 13.12.37	Rk 190 19.10.37	12723 10.02.38	141	DIWE	323	OULTON	U 29.08.36	Rk 94 22.09.36	12622 18.11.36	158	DIWE
281	FULWELL	U 20.12.37	Rk 193 18.01.38	12748 14.03.38	142	DIWE	324	OXTED	U 17.09.36	Rk 95 22.09.36	12632 24.11.36	159	DIWE
282	GLAXY	P 29.01.36	Rk 58 18.02.36	12536 22.06.36	47	DIWE	325	PADBURY	U 07.09.36	Rk 100 20.10.36	12597 27.10.36	160	DIWE
283	GLOSSOR	U 19.02.38	Rk 196 15.03.38	12742 09.03.38	143	9/46 sold	326	PALLAS	K 03.09.35	Br 533 25.09.35	12428 20.11.35	27	DIWE
284	GRETNA	U 14.03.38	Rk 197 15.03.38	12753 15.03.38	144	DIWE	327	PAVO	K 10.07.35	Br 503 24.07.35	12401 15.10.35	69	DIWE
285	GUISELEY	U 05.04.38	Rk 198 19.04.38	12773 07.04.38	145	DIWE	328	PENELOPE	Q 12.01.36	Br 587 24.06.36	12598 28.10.36	77	5/42 JGC
286	HADFIELD	U 19.05.38	Rk 199 20.09.38	12786 13.09.38	146	DIWE	329	PHAETHON	P 04.06.36	Rk 73 16.06.36	12562 26.08.36	68	12/43 LBF
287	HAGLEY	U 11.08.36	Rk 200 20.09.38	Never gauged	147	DIWE	330	PHOEBE	M 14.06.35	Rk 39 18.06.35	12417 25.10.35	72	11/41 S&S
288	HALE	U 28.09.38	Rk 201 25.03.39	Never gauged	148	DIWE	331	PHOSPHORUS	P 13.02.36	Rk 59 18.02.36	12517 13.06.36	51	9/46 sold
289	HALTON	U 00.07.00	Rk 71 21.07.36	12597 27.09.36	149	DIWE	332	PICTOR	K 17.07.35	Br 507 24.07.35	12451 29.11.35	70	DIWE
290	HEBE	P 13.02.36	Rk 61 17.03.36	12481 24.03.36	54	1/41 AWL	333	PLEIADES	Q 06.12.35	Br 586 26.02.36	12576 29.08.36	76	DIWE
291	HECTOR	P 23.11.35	Rk 51 05.11.35	12470 12.03.36	43	8/42 AWL	334	POLARIS	K 08.08.35	Br 519 03.09.35	12410 23.10.35	85	9/47 MSC
292	HYADES	K 15.05.35	Br 515 03.09.35	12449 28.11.35	53	DIWE	335	POLLUX	M 27.04.35	Rk 37 21.05.35	12521 15.06.36	24	1/44 LMS
293	HYDRUS	K 08.07.35	Br 497 24.07.35	12539 22.06.36	52	12/43 LBF	336	POPLAR	U 19.09.36	Rk 101 20.10.36	12586 21.10.36	161	DIWE
294	INDUS	K 23.07.35	Br 509 03.09.35	12388 09.10.35	71	DIWE	337	PRINCESS	E 21.07.31	Tr 115 01.09.31	12314 14.04.32	78	DIWE
295	JUNO	K 29.08.35	Br 531 03.09.35	12473 13.03.36	96	DIWE	338	PROSPERITY	A 12.11.30	Dv 418 02.12.30	X5589 17.03.26	2	scrapped
296	KEW	U 09.07.36	Rk 75 21.07.36	12579 19.10.36	150	DIWE	339	PUPPIS	L 11.05.35	B 1575 20.09.35	12455 05.03.36	73	DIWE
297	KNEBWORTH	U 18.07.36	Rk 77 21.07.36	12630 23.11.36	151	DIWE	340	PURLEY	U 30.09.36	Rk 102 20.10.36	12615 07.11.36	162	9/46 FSC
298	LAMBOURNE	U 18.07.36	Rk 78 21.07.36	12640 30.11.36	152	7/46 sold	341	RA	P 06.12.35	Rk 53 08.01.36	12505 09.06.36	44	3/41 S&S
299	LANGHO	U 01.08.36	Rk 82 11.08.36	12575 28.08.36	154	DIWE	342	RAWDON	U 24.10.36	Rk 103 20.10.36	12600 28.10.36	163	DIWE
300	LEO	L 22.07.35	Br 535 25.09.35	12453 04.03.36	42	DIWE	343	REGULUS	O 14.11.35	B 1590 19.06.36	12483 24.03.36	79	9/42 GUC
301	LEONIDS	O 04.06.36	Rk 141 16.03.37	12593 24.10.36	100	9/42 GUC	344	RIGAL	N 20.12.35	Br 585 22.01.36	12500 08.06.36	36	DIWE
302	LEPUS	L 04.07.35	Br 521 03.09.35	12554 24.08.36	57	1/47 MSC	345	ROADE	U 25.11.36	Rk 105 15.12.36	12634 26.11.36	164	DIWE
303	LICHFIELD	U 01.08.36	Rk 81 11.08.36	12591 23.10.36	153	DIWE	346	ROMSEY	U 16.11.36	Rk 106 15.12.36	12624 20.11.36	165	DIWE
304	LUPUS	L 22.01.36	B 1593 19.06.36	12464 10.03.36	8	1/47 MSC	347	RUGBY	A 31.03.33	Dv 442 18.04.33	12023 25.06.20	48	DIWE
305	LYNX	L 30.10.35	Rk 120 15.12.36	12430 21.11.35	19	DIWE	348	RUISLIP	U 12.11.36	Rk 107 15.12.36	12620 16.11.36	166	DIWE

No	Name	Builder/Date	Registered	Gauged	Pair	Fate	No	Name	Builder/Date	Registered	Gauged	Pair	Fate
349	SALTLEY	U 28.11.36	Rk 108 15.12.36	12636 27.11.36	167	DIWE	369	TAUNTON	U 03.03.37	Rk 142 16.03.37	12704 09.03.37	182	DIWE
350	SARPEDON	O 17.03.36	Rk 188 21.09.37	12535 20.06.36	84	9/42 GUC	370	TAURUS	O 07.05.36	B 1594 19.06.36	12519 15.06.36	92	11/45 GUC
351	SATELLITE	K 26.09.35	Br 543 23.10.35	12460 06.03.36	87	DIWE	371	TAYPORT	U 03.03.37	Rk 139 16.03.37	12737 17.02.38	181	DIWE
352	SATURN	H 25.11.34	Tr 125 01.01.35	12376 26.03.35	95	11/45 GUC	372	THEA	O 19.04.36	B 1597 17.07.36	12607 05.11.36	91	9/42 GUC
353	SCALES	O 07.01.36	Rk 191 19.10.37	12493 27.03.36	83	9/42 GUC	373	THOTH	O 14.05.36	B 1602 18.12.36	12502 08.06.36	93	9/42 GUC
354	SEASCALE	U 15.01.37	Rk 109 15.12.36	12727 11.02.38	168	DIWE	374	TILBURY	U 10.02.37	Rk 137 16.03.37	12660 12.02.37	179	DIWE
355	SERPENS	L 20.06.35	Br 527 03.09.35	12396 11.10.35	80	DIWE	375	TITANIA	K 18.05.35	Br 511 03.09.35	12394 11.10.35	90	DIWE
356	SHAMROCK	A 20.02.34	Tr 118 20.02.34	X5456 22.10.09	86	scrapped	376	TIVERTON	U 10.02.37	Rk 138 16.03.37	12662 12.02.37	180	DIWE
357	SHILTON	U 26.11.36	Rk 110 15.12.36	12647 02.12.36	169	DIWE	377	TOUCAN	L 29.11.35	B 1585 15.05.36	12498 06.06.36	82	DIWE
358	SIRIUS	I 24.10.34	Rk 29 20.11.34	12357 11.02.35	13	6/43 LMS	378	TRIAGULUM	O 02.04.36	B 1586 19.06.36	12528 17.06.36	89	9/42 GUC
359	SLINFOLD	U 03.12.36	Rk 112 15.12.36	12697 05.03.37	170	DIWE	379	TYDD	U 04.03.37	Rk 143 16.03.37	12739 21.02.38	183	DIWE
360	SOUTHAM	U 05.01.37	Rk 116 15.12.36	12686 25.02.37	171	DIWE	380	URANUS	K 21.08.35	Br 529 03.09.35	12486 25.03.36	75	7/47 HDE
361	SPICA	I 05.03.35	Rk 34 19.03.35	12372 12.03.35	7	6/43 SBC	381	URSA	M 21.08.35	Rk 45 17.09.35	12408 23.10.35	94	2/41 AWL
362	STARCROSS	U 11.02.37	Rk 117 15.12.36	12670 17.02.37	172	DIWE	382	UTTOXETER	U 30.03.37	Rk 145 20.04.37	Never gauged	184	DIWE
363	STAVERTON	U 23.02.37	Rk 124 19.01.37	12695 04.03.37	173	DIWE	383	VELA	K 04.07.35	Br 492 24.07.35	12398 12.10.35	98	DIWE
364	STOULTON	U 22.12.36	Rk 123 19.01.37	12651 09.02.37	174	DIWE	384	VIRGINIS	K 21.09.35	Br 541 25.09.35	12439 26.11.35	50	DIWE
365	STREATHAM	U 05.01.37	Rk 125 19.01.37	12693 03.03.37	175	DIWE	385	WIVENHOE	U 21.04.37	Rk 146 20.04.37	12765 24.03.38	185	DIWE
366	SUNBURY	U 05.01.37	Rk 127 19.01.37	12730 12.02.38	176	DIWE	386	YEOVIL	U 12.04.37	Rk 148 20.04.37	12745 10.03.38	186	DIWE
367	SURBITON	U 11.02.37	Rk 131 16.02.37	12678 22.02.37	177	DIWE	387	ZENITH	P 16.05.36	Rk 69 19.05.36	12511 10.06.36	64	9/42 JGC
368	TAPLOW	U 29.01.37	Rk 132 16.02.37	12712 17.03.37	178	DIWE	388	(MARY)	B 02.02.29	Tr 109 05.02.29	12181 25.02.29	46	4/36 GUC

KEY TO BUILDERS AND CONSTRUCTION

ASSOCIATED CANAL CARRIERS
A   5 wooden motors 6 wooden butties & one iron composite butty (RUGBY) from other carriers.

ROYALTY CLASS
B   The prototype steel pair built by the Steel Barrel Co. Ltd. at Uxbridge, Middlesex with wooden cabins built by Bushell Brothers of Tring.

C   4 coppered-steel motor boat hulls built by W. J. Yarwood & Sons Ltd. at Northwich, Cheshire.

D   2 coppered-steel motor boats built by James Pollock Sons & Co. Ltd. at Faversham, Kent.

E   2 wooden butties built by Bushell Brothers at Tring, Hertfordshire.

F   2 wooden butties built by W.H. Walker & Brothers Ltd. at Rickmansworth, Hertfordshire.

G   2 wooden butties built by Edward G. Woods at Staffordshire Wharf, Brentford, Middlesex.

STAR CLASS
H   2 prototype wooden pairs built by Harland & Wolff Ltd. at its Woolwich Shipyard but with the cabin work by Bushells.

I   3 prototype wooden pairs built by Walkers.

J   1 prototype wooden pair built by Edward Woods at Brentford.

K   24 iron-composite pairs built by Harland & Wolff. (Small Woolwich)

L   12 iron-composite pairs built by Yarwoods. (Small Northwich)

M   6 wooden pairs built by Walkers (Small Ricky)

N   18 steel-composite pairs built by Harland & Wolff. (Small Woolwich)

O   8 steel pairs with "Vee" bottoms built by Yarwoods. (Middle Northwich)

P   12 wooden pairs built by Walkers. (Small Ricky)

Q   2 wooden pairs built by Woods.

TOWN CLASS
R   24 steel pairs built by Harland & Wolff. (Large Woolwich)

S   24 steel motors built by Harland & Wolff. (Large Woolwich)

T   38 steel motors built by Yarwoods. (Large Northwich)

U   62 wooden butties built by Walkers. (Large Ricky)

KEY TO REGISTRATIONS & GAUGINGS

B	City of Birmingham
Br	Brentford
Cv	Coventry
Dv	Daventry
Rk	Rickmansworth
Tm	Tamworth
Tr	Tring

X before gauging denotes Oxford Canal number
* denotes registration for previous owner

KEY TO MAIN DISPOSALS

AWL	A. Wander Ltd., Kings Langley, Hertfordshire (manufacturers of Ovaltine)
DIWE	Docks & Inland Waterways Executive (British Waterways)
FSC	Flixborough Shipping Co. Ltd., Horninglow, Staffordshire
GUC	Grand Union Canal Company (the parent concern of the GUCCC)
HDE	H. Dean, Manchester
JGC	John Green (Carriers) Ltd., Macclesfield, Cheshire
LBF	Lawrence Boyd Faulkner, Leighton Buzzard, Bedfordshire
LMS	London Midland & Scottish Railway Company
MOWT	Ministry of War Transport (requisitioned)
MSC	Manchester Ship Canal Company (Bridgewater Department)
RSCB	River Severn Catchment Board
S&S	Stanton & Staveley Ltd., Stanton Ironworks, Derbyshire
SBC	Samuel Barlow Coal Co. Ltd., Birmingham & Braunston
SEB	Samuel Edwin Barlow, Tamworth, Staffordshire
TCP	Thomas Clayton (Paddington) Ltd.
TGC	Talbot Garage Company, Kidderminster, Worcestershire
TSE	T. & S. Element Ltd., Birmingham

KEY TO OTHER DISPOSALS

MOTORS

2	ADVANCE	Damaged by a bomb and never repaired - scrapped 1940
19	BELLATRIX	7/42 sold to Wulfruna Coal Co, Wolverhampton, £825
21	CALLISTO	4/47 sold to G. H. Lupton, £450
46	GEORGE	4/36 became a maintenance boat on the Regent's Canal.
48	(THE) HAWK	3/36 sold to Hubert Coles, £130; in 1940 passed to S.E. Barlow.
51	HESPERUS	7/47 sold to Lord Bingham, £400; in 1953 became John Knill's CHAD
55	JOSEPHINE M'	8/39 sold to Edward Wood, Bedworth, £80
58	LIBRA	4/47 sold to E. Worley; in 1954 became Willow Wren's WARBLER
75	PLATO	2/41 sold to E. Probert & Sons, .£650; in 1949 Elements PRINCESS ANNE.
99	WILLIAM	11/47 sold to J. Goddard, £300

BUTTIES

209	ALTAIR	9/46 sold to George Garside, Leighton Buzzard £231; later reverted to DIWE
228	BARRHEAD	11/47 sold to Thomas Burton Ltd., £480.
262	COUNT	5/44 sold to steerer Whitehouse, £50.
273	DUCHESS	7/45 sold to the Northampton Sea Scouts, £105.
276	ELSIE EDITH	Scrapped about 1938
283	GLOSSOR	9/46 sold to G. D. Sawyer, £325.
298	LAMBOURNE	7/46 sold to Richard C March, Whittington Grange, Worcester, £300.
331	PHOSPHORUS	9/46 sold to Robert Fordyce Aickman, £264.
338	PROSPERITY	Scrapped about 1939
356	SHAMROCK	Scrapped about 1939
388	MARY	4/36 became a maintenance boat.

GENERAL NOTES

13	ARCTURUS - numbered 12A in practice to overcome superstitions
38	DUKE - also registered as Dv 450 15.05.34
41	ENCELADUS - also registered as Br 538 25.09.35
48	THE HAWK - also registered as Dv 453 15.05.34
55	Full name is JOSEPHINE MARGUERITE
85	Full name is SOUTHERN CROSS
108	BADSEY - also registered as Rk 165 20.07.37
226	BANBURY - also registered as Rk 162 15.06.37
262	COUNT - also registered as Rk 55 08.01.36
263	COUNTESS - also registered as Rk 56 18.02.36
273	DUCHESS - also registered as Dv 449 15.05.34
282	Probably intended to be named GALAXY
287	HAGLEY - delivery date estimated
288	HALE - delivery date estimated
306	LYRA - also registered as Br 539 25.09.35
331	PHOSPHORUS - built with a fore cabin to accommodate the boatman's two grown-up sons
347	RUGBY - also registered as Dv 454 12.06.34
378	Probably intended to be named TRIANGULUM
388	MARY was never part of the official GUCCC fleet.

SCHEDULE OF DELIVERIES OF NEW BOATS

HARLAND & WOLFF LIMITED, WOOLWICH.

H 2 prototype wooden pairs (cabin work by Bushell Brothers of Tring) ordered 24 April 1934.

25.11.34 VENUS & SATURN; 2.01.35 ALDEBARAN & ORION.

K 24 composite pairs with iron sides & elm bottoms ordered 10 January 1935 at £1,275 per pair.

15 05.35 HYPERION & HYADES; 18.05.35 THEMIS & TITANIA; 12.06.35 CENTAURI & CETUS; 14.06.35 AURIGA & ARGO; 21.06.35 CEPHEUS & CYGNUS; AQUILA & ARA; 29.06.35 CASSIOPEIA & CRUX; 4.07.35 VIRGO & VELA; 8.07.35 HYDRA & HYDRUS; 10.07.35 PEGASUS & PAVO, CAPRICORN & CRATER; 17.07.35 PERSEUS & PICTOR; 23.07.35 PHOBOS & INDUS; 29.07.35 GEMINI & ARGUS; 8.08.35 SOUTHERN CROSS & POLARIS; 14.08.35 SUN & MOON; 17.08.35 COMET & METEOR; 21.08.35 PLATO & URANUS; 29.08.35 VESTA & JUNO; 3.09.35 CERES & PALLAS; 13.09.35 MERCURY & ASTRAEA; 21.09.35 HERCULES & VIRGINIS; 26.09.35 STAR & SATELLITE; 4.10.35 PLANET & NEBULAE.

N 18 composite pairs with mild steel sides & elm bottoms ordered 3 May 1935 at £1,276 per pair.

30.10.35 ACHERNAR & ACTIS; 1.11.35 ALCOR & ALPHONS; 8.11.35 ALGOL & ARGON

30.10.35 ACHERNAR & ACTIS; 1.11.35 ALCOR & ALPHONS; 8.11.35 ALGOL & ARGON, ANTONY & CLEOPATRA; 16.11.35 AQUARIUS & ANDROMEDA, ARCAS & AURORA; 23.11.35 ARCHIMEDES & MARCELLUS, ASTEROPE & ACHILLES; 29.11.35 ATLAS & ATALANTA, BARGUS & BETELGEUSE; 6.12.35 BOOTES & BELLEROPHON, CALLISTO & CAPELLA; 16.12.35 COLUMBA & DODONA, COROLLA & CANIS, CORONA & CORONIS; 20.12.35 DEIMOS & DIPPER, DENEBOLA & DUBHE, DORADO & RIGAL.

R 24 pairs of all mild steel construction ordered 29 January 1936 at £1,363.25 per pair. (7 butties were delivered separately before their intended motors).

16.07.36 ABER & ALPERTON; 28.07.36 ALTON & ABOYNE; 8.08.36 ALDGATE & ANGEL (28/07); 18.08.36 ASCOT & ASTON (8/08); AYNHO & AYR (8/08); 27.08.36 BALDOCK & BANBURY, BANSTEAD & BALHAM; 8.09.36 BADSEY & BARNES, BARNET & BARRHEAD; 18.09.36 BAINTON & BERKHAMSTEAD, BATH & BAWTRY; 2.10.36 BATTERSEA & BAYSWATER, BEAULIEU & BEDWORTH; 15.10.36 BARNHAM & BELMONT, BELFAST & BAILDON, BEXHILL & BEVERLEY; 30.10.36 BICESTER & BIDEFORD, BILSTER & BINGLEY; 17.11.36 BLETCHLEY & BAKEWELL (30/10), BOGNOR & BODMIN, BIRMINGHAM & BORDESLEY; 12.12.36 BOURNEMOUTH & BRANKSOME (17/11), BRISTOL & BRIGHTON (27/11), BUCKEN & BUDE (27/11).

S 24 motors of all steel construction ordered 11 March 1936 at £900 each.

16.07.36 BARROW; 28.07.36 BUXTON; 8.08.36 CALDY; 29.12.36 CALSTOCK, CAMBOURNE; 29.01.37 CHERTSEY, CHISWICK, COLESHILL, CANTLEY, CARNABY, DARLEY; 26.02.37 DOVER, DUNSTABLE, EDGWARE, ELSTREE; 14.03.37 GREENLAW; 24.03.37 EPSOM, FENNY, FULBOURNE, GAINSBOROUGH; 05.04.37 HAMPSTEAD; 23.04.37 GREENOCK; 19.05.37 HADLEY, HAWKESBURY.

WJ YARWOOD & SONS LIMITED, NORTHWICH

C 4 copper-bearing-steel hulls ordered by ACC on 26 March 1931 at £2,365.

16.10.31 DUKE; VICTORIA; 30.11.31 EDWARD; WILLIAM.

L 12 composite pairs with iron sides and elm bottoms ordered 10 January 1935 at £1,250 per pair.

11.05.35 PISCES & PUPPIS; 6.06.35 CLYPEUS & CORVUS; 20.06.35 SAGITTA & SERPENS; 4.07.35 LACERTA & LEPUS; 22.07.35 ERIDANUS & LEO; 21.08.35 ENCELADUS & LYRA; 19.09.35 DELPHINUS & DRACO; 4.10.35 SCORPIO & MALUS; 16.10.35 LIBRA & CARINA; 30.10.35 BELLATRIX & LYNX; 29.11.35 SCULPTOR & TOUCAN; 22.01.36 ANTLIA & LUPUS.

O 8 pairs of all steel construction with Vee bottoms ordered 3 May 1935 at £1,301 per pair.

14.11.35 RADIANT & REGULUS; 7.01.36 SEXTANS & SCALES; 17.03.36 SICKLE & SARPEDON; 2.04.36 TAYGETA & TRIAGULUM; 19.04.36 THEOPHILUS & THEA; 7.05.36 TUCANA & TAURUS; 14.05.36 TYCHO & THOTH; 4.06.36 ZODIAC & LEONIDS.

T 38 motors of all steel construction ordered 11 March 1936 at £900 each.

30.06.36 HALSALL, KENILWORTH; 10.07.36 KELSO, LADYBANK; 22.07.36 LETCHWORTH, LANCING; 8.08.36 NABURN, NUNEATON; 18.08.36 NUTFIELD, OTLEY; 22.08.36 OAKLEY; 4.09.36 PADDINGTON, PINNER; 10.09.36 PURTON; 7.10.36 READING, RENTON; 13.10.36 RENFREW, RUFFORD; 24.10.36 SALTAIRE, SEAFORD; 29.10.36 SHIRLEY, SLOUGH; 19.11.36 STAMFORD, STANTON; 21.11.36 SOUTHALL, STIRLING; 15.12.36 STRATFORD, SUDBURY, SUTTON; 12.01.37 TADWORTH; 15.01.37 THAXTED, TIPTON; 15.02.37 TOWCESTER, TARPORLEY; 8.03.37 TYSELEY, USWORTH; 23.04.37 WHITBY, YEOFORD.

W H WALKER & BROTHERS LIMITED, RICKMANSWORTH.

F 2 wooden butties ordered by ACC on 26 March 1931 at £680.

25.07.31 ADELAIDE, ANNE.

I 3 pairs of wooden boats ordered one at a time on 24 April 1934, 1 June 1934 and 9 November 1934 all at £800 per pair (engines not included).

24.10.34 ARCTURUS & SIRIUS; 18.12.34 NEPTUNE & ALTAIR; 5.03.35 ANTARES & SPICA.

M 6 pairs with oak sides & elm bottoms ordered 10 January 1935 at £790 per pair (engines not included).

27.04.35 CASTOR & POLLUX; 14.06.35 PHOENIX & PHOEBE; 6.07.35 ARIES & ARIEL; 2.08.35 OBERON & OCTANS; 21.08.35 UMBRIEL & URSA; 12.09.35 MIMAS & MUSCA.

P 12 pairs with oak sides & elm bottoms ordered 3 May 1935 at £1,128 each complete.

23.10.35 ELECTRA & ETHIOPIA; 23.11.35 FOMALHAUT & HECTOR; 6.12.35 FORNAX & RA; 29.01.36 GRUS & GLAXY; 13.02.36 HESPERUS & PHOSPHORUS, ISIS & HEBE; 10.03.36 MAIA & MEDUSA; 9.04.36 MEROPE & MERAK; 16.05.36 MIRA & MILKY WAY, MIZAR & ZENITH; 25.05.36 MONOCEROS & MARFAK; 4.06.36 ORPHEUS & PHAETHON.

U 62 butties with oak sides & elm bottoms ordered 11 March 1936 at £390 each.

9.07.36 HALTON, KEW; 18.07.36 KNEBWORTH, LAMBOURNE; 20.07.36 BURY; 30.07.36 BYFIELD; 1.08.36 LICHFIELD, LANGHO; 12.08.36 NORTON, NUNHEAD; 18.08.36 CARDIFF; 29.08.36 NESTON, OULTON; 7.09.36 PADBURY; 17.09.36 OXTED; 19.09.36 POPLAR; 30.09.36 PURLEY; 24.10.36 RAWDON; 12.11.36 RUISLIP; 16.11.36 ROMSEY; 25.11.36 ROADE; 26.11.36 SHILTON; 28.11.36 SALTLEY; 3.12.36 SLINFOLD; 22.12.36 STOULTON; 5.01.37 SOUTHAM, STREATHAM, SUNBURY; 15.01.37 SEASCALE; 29.01.37 TAPLOW; 10.02.37 TILBURY, TIVERTON; 11.02.37 STARCROSS, SURBITON; 23.02.37 STAVERTON; 3.03.37 TAYPORT, TAUNTON; 4.03.37 TYDD; 30.03.37 UTTOXETER; 12.04.37 YEOVIL; 21.04.37 WIVENHOE; 22.04.37 CHALFONT; 6.05.37 CHEAM; 10.05.37 CHESHAM; 18.05.37 CHIPSTEAD; 29.05.37 COBHAM; 05.06.37 CONISTON; 12.06.37 DENTON; 28.06.37 COUGHTON; 29.07.37 DOWNHAM; 6.08.37 DUDLEY; 18.09.37 EALING; 4.12.37 ELTON, EWELL; 13.12.37 FELTHAM; 20.12.37 FULWELL; 19.02.38 GLOSSOR; 14.03.38 GRETNA; 5.04.38 GUISELEY; 19.05.38 HADFIELD; 11.08.38 HAGLEY; 28.09.38 HALE.

EDWARD G WOODS, STAFFORDSHIRE WHARF, BRENTFORD.

G 2 wooden butties ordered by ACC on 26 March 1931 for £660.
16.06.31 DUCHESS; 20.10.31 ALEXANDRA.

J 1 wooden pair with oak sides & elm bottoms ordered on 24 April 1934 for £655 without an engine
4.12.34 JUPITER & MARS

Q 2 wooden pairs ordered on 3 May 1935 at £1,006 per pair complete.
6.12.35 PLEIONE & PLEIADES; 12.01.36 PRAESEPE & PENELOPE

JAMES POLLOCK SONS & COMPANY LIMITED, FAVERSHAM.

D 2 motors of copper-bearing steel with 20hp Bolinders ordered by ACC on 26 March 1931 at £1,896.
15.07.31 HENRY, PRINCE.

BUSHELL BROTHERS, TRING

E 2 wooden butties ordered by ACC on 26 March 1931 at £760.
21.07.31 PRINCESS; 23.11.31 ALBERT.

STEEL BARREL COMPANY LIMITED, UXBRIDGE

B One experimental pair of steel boats (wooden cabin work by Bushells Brothers of Tring) ordered by the Regent's Canal & Dock Company on 20 July 1928 at £870 without the engine.
02.02.29 GEORGE & MARY

BOATS ACQUIRED BY ASSOCIATED CANAL CARRIERS LIMITED

MOTOR BOATS

ADVANCE Built at the end of 1914 as PIONEER for the U.K. Motor Transport Co. Ltd. (Brentford 339 - 19.01.15; GJC 11888 - 18.01.15). Passed to the Red Star Motor Co. Ltd. and renamed ARETHUSA (Brentford 376 - 20.08.18, intended traffic cocoa beans). Passed to John Walker of Bugbrooke from whom ACC purchased her and butty PROSPERITY in November 1930 for £360. ADVANCE was war damaged in 1940 and scrapped.

DORNEY COURT Built 1928 at Polesworth as a horse boat for John Brookes of Bedworth and named after a Great Western Railway locomotive (Tamworth 45 - 07.04.28; OC 5615 - 27.04.28). Converted to a motor at Braunston in 1930 (Daventry 405 - 25.03.30, new cabin) and sold to ACC with ELSIE EDITH in January 1935 for £450. DORNEY COURT was sold to S. E. Barlow of Tamworth in June 1941 for £275 and renamed ARK ROYAL (Tamworth 182 - 06.09.41).

HAWK Built 1927 as SENTINEL at Taylor's yard at Chester for Charles Payne Crofts of Northampton and equipped with a Sentinel steam lorry engine and boiler (Chester 822 - 13.09.27). In 1928 Payne Crofts formed Midland Canal Transport at Northampton to which SENTINEL passed, being converted to a motor and renamed HAWK (Daventry 382 - 28.02.28; OC 5614 - 29.02.28). ACC was incorporated on 28 January 1929 to take over Midland Canal Transport and so acquired HAWK, which was renamed THE HAWK (Daventry 398 - 18.06.29). ACC sold THE HAWK on 19 March 1936 to Hubert Coles for £130 who soon passed her to John Thomas Coles of Thrupp (Daventry 486 - 07.06.37; OC 5614 - 17.03.38). She then passed to S. E. Barlow of Tamworth (Tamworth 173 - 02.11.40) and subsequently to John Walley of Stoke on Trent (Tamworth 202 - 23.04.49). Walley sold her to Mr. Roy Mack in April 1953 for conversion.

JOSEPHINE MARGUERITE Built 1927 by Walkers at Rickmansworth for the Honourable Rupert Craven of Wadley Manor, Faringdon, Berkshire (Rickmansworth 6 - 08.09.27, captain Joseph Coles; OC 5612 - 08.12.27) and sold to ACC in October 1932 for £215 with COOMBE ABBEY for £80. JOSEPHINE MARGUERITE was sold to George Wood of Polesworth on 19 August 1939 for £80 by which time her value in the GUCCC's books was virtually nil. Wood renamed her UNION JACK (Tamworth 170 -02.11.40) and then sold her to S.E. Barlow of Tamworth (Tamworth 185 - 19.09.42). The S.E. Barlow fleet was acquired by the Samuel Barlow Coal Co. Ltd. of Birmingham and Braunston in February 1957 when UNION JACK became No 45 in its fleet. She was sold to R. H. Strong in March 1960 probably for conversion.

SPEEDY An early motor built in 1912 by Walkers at Rickmansworth for Emanuel Smith of Brentford (Brentford 320 - 17.12.12; GJC 11781 - 29.01.14); acquired by the Hon. Rupert Craven of Faringdon in 1930 and sold to ACC in February 1934 for £224. SPEEDY was the only ACC motor that passed to the Docks & Inland Waterways Executive on 1 Jan 1948.

BUTTY BOATS

COOMBE ABBEY Built 1927 probably by Sephtons at Tusses Bridge for the Hon. Rupert Craven (Coventry 508 - 05.05.27; OC 5599 - 27.06.27) and sold to ACC with JOSEPHINE MARGUERITE in October 1932. The GUCCC sold COOMBE ABBEY to S. E. Barlow of Tamworth in November 1941 for £70 (her book value being just one penny); she was renamed CUNNINGHAM (Tamworth 183 - 27.12.41).

COUNT Built in February 1926 as No 4 for Bell's United Asbestos Co. Ltd. of Harefield (GJC 12131 - 27.09.26) and sold to ACC in February 1934 together with COUNTESS for £229 the pair. COUNT was sold to ex steerer Whitehouse in May 1944 for £50.

COUNTESS Built in September 1926 as No 5 for Bell's United Asbestos Co. Ltd. of Harefield (GJC 12130 - 23.09.26) and sold to ACC in February 1934 together with COUNT for £229 the pair. COUNTESS was only one of the two ACC butties that passed to the Docks & Inland Waterways Executive on 1 January 1948.

ELSIE EDITH Built 1908 by Nursers at Braunston as WASHFORD for the Oxford Portland Cement Company of Kirtlington (Daventry 265 - 23.09.08; OC 5439 - 25.09.08). Purchased by John Wilson and renamed FORGET ME NOT (Tamworth 64 - 09.03.29; OC 5439 - 23.03.29) and then by John Brookes of Bedworth and renamed ELSIE EDITH (Tamworth 104 - 19.09.1931; OC 5439 - 16.11.31). Sold to ACC with DORNEY COURT. ELSIE EDITH was scrapped by the GUCCC probably in the late 1930s, the Tamworth register entry being cancelled on 24 May 1938.

PROSPERITY Previous history not known but rebuilt 1925 by Nursers of Braunston for John Walker of Banbury (Daventry 370 - 18.08.25; OC 5589 - 17.03.26) and sold to ACC with ADVANCE. PROSPERITY was scrapped by the GUCCC probably in the late 1930s.

RUGBY Built 1913 by Braithwaite & Kirk of West Bromwich for Fellows, Morton & Clayton Limited (Birmingham 1300 - 03.10.13; BCN 22735 - 12.07.17; GJC 12023 - 25.06.20) and sold to ACC in March 1933 for £85. RUGBY was the other ACC butty to pass to the Docks & Inland Waterways Executive on 1 January 1948.

SHAMROCK Built 1909 by Nursers at Braunston as KIRTLINGTON for the Oxford Portland Cement Company of Kirtlington (Daventry 275 - 08.09.09; OC 5456 - 22.10.09). Acquired by John George Grantham of Banbury and renamed SHAMROCK (Daventry 389 - 29.01.29; OC 5456 - 20.01.29). Purchased by Bushell Brothers of Tring (Tring 118 - 07.06.32) and sold to ACC in February 1934 for £95 after reconditioning. SHAMROCK was scrapped by the GUCCC probably in the late 1930s.

ASSOCIATED CANAL CARRIERS BOATS (not passing to the GUCCC)

DOROTHY Previous history not known. Registered Daventry 397 - 18.06.29. Sold to the Grand Union Canal Company in December 1931 for £45.

DOVE Built 1906 by Fellows Morton & Clayton Ltd. at Uxbridge as MONMOUTH (Uxbridge 381 - 31.07.06; GJC 12093 - 05.03.23; BCN 20117 - 06.12.06). Sold to Nursers in July 1927 for £35 and renamed RAY (Daventry 376 - 13.09.27). Sold to MCT (Daventry 381 - 28.02.28) and passed to ACC in July 1929 (Daventry 401 - 13.08.29) who gifted her back to Nursers in December 1931.

OWL Built as BULGARIA for the Shropshire Union Railways & Canal Company (Chester 776 - 05.10.15), sold to Charles Payne Crofts in 1927 and renamed EVER WATCHFUL (Chester 823 - 13.09.27) to serve as a butty to SENTINEL. On formation of Midland Canal Transport EVER WATCHFUL became OWL (Daventry 383 - 28.02.28) and on passing to ACC became THE OWL (Daventry 396 - 18.06.29) but was sold in April 1933 for £25.

ROOK Built 1900 by Nursers at Braunston as MONTAGUE for Charles Nelson & Co. Ltd. of Stockton. (Paddington 206 - 16.10.00; GJC 10988 - 01.05.00; BCN 20831 - 12.03.09). Sold to Nursers and renamed HILDA (Daventry 352 - 12.12.22). Sold to W. H. Sephton, Tusses Bridge (Coventry 507 - 05.05.27). Sold to E. Kendall (Daventry 379 - 08.11.27) who sold her to ACC where she was renamed THE ROOK (Daventry 395 - 18.06.29). She was sold to the Grand Union Canal Company in December 1931 for £35.

SALLIE Ex Harris Brothers, Brierley Hill (GUC 11686 - 27.02.11). Passed to Noah Hingley & Sons Ltd (Brierley Hill 288 - 07.03.21) and then to Midlands & Coast Canal Carriers Ltd. Passed to ACC (Daventry 392 - 23.04.29). Gifted to steerer Wenlock in December 1931.

TARZAN Ex Price & Son, Brierley Hill. Passed to Midlands & Coast Canal Carriers Ltd (Wolverhampton 1109 - 26.09.27). Passed to ACC (Daventry 391 - 23.04.29). Gifted to steerer H. Wenlock in December 1931 (GJC 11963 - 09.05.32).

BOATS SURVIVING TO PASS TO THE DOCKS & INLAND WATERWAYS EXECUTIVE on 1 January 1948 following nationalisation.

This list was reproduced in *"Canals"* by H. Newton, published by Ian Allan Limited in 1948.

MOTOR BOATS

1	ACHERNAR	79	RADIANT	122	BOURNEMOUTH	156	NUNEATON
4	ALCOR	80	SAGITTA	123	BRISTOL	157	NUTFIELD
6	ANTONY	81	SCORPIO	124	BUCKDEN	158	OTLEY
8	ANTLIA	82	SCULPTOR	125	BARROW	159	OAKLEY
9	AQUARIUS	85	SOUTHERN X	126	BUXTON	160	PADDINGTON
10	AQUILA	86	SPEEDY	127	CALDY	161	PINNER
11	ARCAS	87	STAR	128	CAMBOURNE	162	PURTON
15	ASTEROPE	88	SUN	129	CALSTOCK	163	READING
16	ATLAS	89	TAYGETA	130	CHERTSEY	165	RENFREW
17	AURIGA	90	THEMIS	131	CHISWICK	166	RUFFORD
18	BARGUS	92	TUCANA	132	COLESHILL	167	SALTAIRE
20	BOOTES	98	VIRGO	133	CANTLEY	168	SEAFORD
22	CAPRICORN	100	ZODIAC	134	CARNABY	169	SHIRLEY
23	CASSIOPEIA	101	ABER	135	DARLEY	170	SLOUGH
25	CENTAURI	102	ALTON	136	DOVER	171	SOUTHALL
28	CLYPEUS	103	ALDGATE	138	EDGWARE	172	STAMFORD
30	COMET	104	ASCOT	139	ELSTREE	173	STANTON
31	COROLLA	105	AYNHO	141	FENNY	174	STIRLING
33	DEIMOS	106	BALDOCK	142	FULBOURNE	175	STRATFORD
35	DENEBOLA	107	BANSTEAD	143	GAINSBOROUGH	176	SUDBURY
36	DORADO	108	BADSEY	144	GREENOCK	177	SUTTON
41	ENCELADUS	109	BARNET	145	GREENLAW	178	TADWORTH
42	ERIDANUS	110	BAINTON	146	HAMPSTEAD	179	THAXTED
43	FOMALHAUT	112	BATTERSEA	147	HADLEY	180	TIPTON
45	GEMINI	113	BEAULIEU	148	HAWKESBURY	181	TOWCESTER
52	HYDRA	114	BARNHAM	149	HALSALL	182	TARPORLEY
57	LACERTA	115	BELFAST	150	KENILWORTH	183	TYSELEY
69	PEGASUS	116	BEXHILL	151	KELSO	184	USWORTH
70	PERSEUS	117	BICESTER	152	LADYBANK	185	WHITBY
71	PHOBOS	119	BLETCHLEY	153	LETCHWORTH	186	YEOFORD
73	PISCES	120	BOGNOR	154	LANCING		
76	PLEIONE	121	BIRMINGHAM	155	NABURN		

BUTTY BOATS

201	ABOYNE	242	BRIGHTON	286	HADFIELD	344	RIGAL
202	ACHILLES	243	BUDE	287	HAGLEY	345	ROADE
203	ACTIS	244	BURY	288	HALE	346	ROMSEY
207	ALPERTON	245	BYFIELD	289	HALTON	347	RUGBY
208	ALPHONS	247	CAPELLA	292	HYADES	348	RUISLIP
210	ANDROMEDA	248	CARDIFF	294	INDUS	349	SALTLEY
211	ANGEL	249	CARINA	295	JUNO	351	SATELLITE
213	ARA	251	CHALFONT	296	KEW	354	SEASCALE
214	ARGO	252	CHEAM	297	KNEBWORTH	355	SERPENS
215	ARGON	253	CHESHAM	299	LANGHO	357	SHILTON
216	ARGUS	255	CLEOPATRA	300	LEO	359	SLINFOLD
218	ASTON	256	COBHAM	303	LICHFIELD	360	SOUTHAM
219	ASTRAEA	259	CORONIS	305	LYNX	362	STARCROSS
221	AURORA	261	COUGHTON	306	LYRA	363	STAVERTON
222	AYR	263	COUNTESS	307	MALUS	364	STOULTON
223	BAILDON	264	CRATER	308	MARCELLUS	365	STREATHAM
224	BAKEWELL	265	CRUX	310	MARS	366	SUNBURY
225	BALHAM	266	CYGNUS	313	METEOR	367	SURBITON
226	BANBURY	267	DENTON	315	MOON	368	TAPLOW
227	BARNES	268	DIPPER	318	NESTON	369	TAUNTON
229	BAWTRY	269	DODONA	319	NORTON	371	TAYPORT
230	BAYSWATER	270	DOWNHAM	320	NUNHEAD	374	TILBURY
231	BEDWORTH	271	DRACO	323	OULTON	375	TITANIA
232	BELLEROPHON	272	DUBHE	324	OXTED	376	TIVERTON
233	BELMONT	274	DUDLEY	325	PADBURY	377	TOUCAN
234	BERKHAMSTEAD	275	EALING	326	PALLAS	379	TYDD
235	BETELGEUSE	277	ELTON	327	PAVO	382	UTTTOXETER
236	BEVERLEY	279	EWELL	332	PICTOR	383	VELA
237	BIDEFORD	280	FELTHAM	333	PLEIADES	384	VIRGINIS
238	BINGLEY	281	FULWELL	336	POPLAR	385	WIVENHOE
239	BODMIN	282	GLAXY	337	PRINCESS	386	YEOVIL
240	BORDESLEY	284	GRETNA	339	PUPPIS		
241	BRANKSOME	285	GUISELEY	342	RAWDON		

85 Full name is SOUTHERN CROSS

126 boats in all of which only SPEEDY (86) and none of the Royalty Class motors had survived from the oriiginal ACC fleet. The Town Class was intact except for BATH (111), BILSTER (118), DUNSTABLE (137), EPSOM (140) and RENTON (164).

130 butties of which only COUNTESS (263). PRINCESS (337) and RUGBY (347) survived from the ACC fleet. The Town Class again was largely intact except for BARRHEAD (228), CHIPSTEAD (254), CONISTON (257), GLOSSOR (283), LAMBOURNE (298) and PURLEY (340).

DETAILS OF MAIN DISPOSAL OF BOATS prior to 1 January 1948.

STANTON & STAVELEY LIMITED, STANTON IRONWORKS. (Ilkeston registrations)

No & Name	Date sold	(New) Name	New registration	Subsequent history
5 ALGOL	06/40 £950	STANTON 51	Ilk 99 10.11.41	1947 Stewarts & Lloyds
220 ATALANTA	06/40 £400	STANTON 52	Ilk 100 10.11.41	1947 Stewarts & Lloyds
76 PLEIONE	12/40 £760	STANTON 53	Ilk 101 10.11.41	11/41 returned to GUCCC
333 PLEIADES	12/40 £390	STANTON 54	Ilk 102 10.11.41	11/41 returned to GUCCC
59 MAIA	03/41 £760	STANTON 55	Ilk 103 10.11.41	7/47 Joseph Rayner
341 RA	03/41 £390	STANTON 56	Ilk 104 10.11.41	1947 Stewarts & Lloyds
63 MIRA	05/41 £759	STANTON 57	Ilk 105 10.11.41	7/47 Joseph Rayner
322 ORION	05/41 £320½	STANTON 58	Ilk 106 10.11.41	1947 Stewarts & Lloyds
40 ELECTRA	08/41 £759½	STANTON 59	Ilk 107 02.12.41	1947 Stewarts & Lloyds
309 MARFAK	08/41 £390½	STANTON 60	Ilk 108 02.12.41	1947 Stewarts & Lloyds
96 VESTA	11/41 £788	STANTON 61	Ilk 109 05.05.42	1947 Stewarts & Lloyds
246 CANIS	11/41 £512	STANTON 6	Ilk 110 05.05.42	1947 Stewarts & Lloyds
61 MEROPE	11/41 £759½	STANTON 63	Ilk 111 05.05.42	7/47 Joseph Rayner
330 PHEOBE	11/41 £390½	STANTON 64	Ilk 112 05.05.42	1947 Stewarts & Lloyds

A. WANDER LIMITED, OVALTINE WORKS, KINGS LANGLEY.

No & Name	Date sold	(New) Name	New registration	Subsequent history
54 ISIS	01/41 £950	JIMMY	Rk 60 27.01.41	2/51 A. Harvey-Taylor
290 HEBE	01/41 (pair)	RAY	Rk 61 27.01.41	
47 GRUS	02/41 £950	CECIL	Rk 54 27.02.41	
381 URSA	02/41 (pair)	ENID	Rk 45 27.02.41	6/59 Willow Wren COOT
13 ARCTURUS	08/42 £850	ARCTURUS	Not reregistered	8/54 trip boat
291 HECTOR	08/42 (pair)	HECTOR	Rk 51 25.08.42	6/56 Samuel Barlow Coal Co
62 MIMAS	09/43 £650	MIMAS	Rk 46 19.10.43	6/59 Willow Wren EGRET

SAMUEL BARLOW COAL COMPANY LIMITED, BIRMINGHAM & BRAUNSTON.

No & Name	Date sold	(New) Name	New registration	Subsequent history
72 PHOENIX	09/42 £850	CAIRO	Dv 528 15.12.42	sold 5/1961
387 ZENITH	09/42 (pair)	MONTGOMERY	Dv 529 15.12.42	broken up
66 NEPTUNE	04/43 £900	NEPTUNE	Dv 532 06.04.43	12/61 Seymour Roseblade
321 OCTANS	04/43 (pair)	YORK	Dv 533 06.04.43	bow sold, stern broken up
3 ALDEBARAN	06/43 £900	HALIFAX	Dv 535 01.06.43	
361 SPICA	06/43 (pair)	MOSQUITO	Dv 534 01.06.43	sold 8/61
278 ETHIOPIA	11/45 £290	WARWICK	Dv 540 08.01.46	sold 6/51

PHOENIX & ZENITH were originally purchased by John Green (Carriers) Ltd but passed to Barlows almost immediately.

LAWRENCE BOYD FAULKNER, LINSLADE (LEIGHTON BUZZARD)

No & Name	Date sold	(New) Name	New registration	Subsequent history
316 MUSCA	09/43 £275	MERLIN	Rk 47 19.10.43	
292 HYADES	12/43 £375 --	--	Exchanged for HYDRUS	
293 HYDRUS	12/43 -	RAVEN	B 1636 21.12.50	
329 PHAETHON	12/43 £265	KESTREL	Rk 73 18.12.45	
314 MILKY WAY	05/45 £265	CYGNET	Rk 67 16.05.45	
217 ARIEL	11/45 £270	LINNETT	Rk 41 25.06.47	
24 CASTOR	04/47 £270*	ALBATROSS	Rk 36 25.06.47	* without engine
68 ORPHEUS	06/47 £300*	BUZZARD	Rk 72 25.06.47	* without engine
65 MONOC'S	06/47 £300*	SWALLOW	Rk 70 25.06.47	* without engine

SAMUEL EDWIN BARLOW, TAMWORTH

No & Name	Date sold	(New) Name	New registration	Subsequent history
37 DORNEY C.	06/41 £275	ARK ROYAL	Tm 182 06.09.41	
258 COOMBE A.	11/41 £70	CUNNINGHAM	Tm 183 27.12.41	
64 MIZAR	07/47 £760	BLAKE	Tm 198 25.10.47	2/57 Barlow Coal Co.
311 MEDUSA	07/47 (pair)	HARDY	Tm 199 25.10.47	2/57 Barlow Coal Co.
53 HYPERION	11/47	HYPERION	Tm 201 27.11.48	2/57 Barlow Coal Co.
250 CETUS	11/47	CETUS	Ban 18 11.10.48	Coronet Carrying PRINCESS

FLIXBOROUGH SHIPPING COMPANY LIMITED, HORNINGLOW.

No & Name	Date sold	Subsequent history
137 DUNSTABLE	09/46 £932	To John Knill - DUNSTAN
340 PURLEY	09/46 pair	Reverted to British Waterways
140 EPSOM	09/46 £1200	To John Knill - KENELM
257 CONISTON	09/46 (pair)	Reverted to British Waterways
11 BATH	09/46 £883	To Coronet Carrying - PRINCE
254 CHIPSTEAD	09/46 (pair)	Reverted to British Waterways

T. & S. ELEMENT LIMITED, BIRMINGHAM Oldbury registrations

No & Name	Date sold	(New) Name	New registration	Subsequent history
77 PRAESEPE	04/41 £650	MAY QUEEN	Old 10 09.10.41	
94 UMBRIEL	09/41 £660	KING GEORGE	Old 10 09.10.41	
44 FORNAX	11/45 £300*	MAYFLOWER	Old 19 03.07.46	* damaged by fire

JOHN GREEN (CARRIERS) LIMITED, MACCLESFIELD

No & Name	Date sold	(New) Name	New registration
56 JUPITER	05/42 £750	JUPITER	Dv 525 25.08.42
328 PENELOPE	05/42 (pair)	PENELOPE	Dv 526 25.08.42
72 PHOENIX	09/42 £850		
387 ZENITH	09/42 (pair)		

PHOENIX & ZENITH passed almost immediately to the Samuel Barlow Coal Co Ltd.

LONDON MIDLAND & SCOTTISH RAILWAY COMPANY 6/43 OBERON (63) & SIRIUS (358) £1,165, 1/44 ARIES (14) & POLLUX (335) £1,200, 6/46 HERCULES (50) & NEBULAE (317) £875.

TALBOT GARAGE COMPANY, KIDDERMINSTER 6/42 DELPHINUS (34) £470 later became Elements PRINCE CHARLES; 7/42 ANTARES (7) registered as Kidderminster 318 and re-named ANTRIES.

MANCHESTER SHIP CANAL COMPANY (BRIDGEWATER DEPARTMENT) 1/47 LEPUS (302) £280, 1/47 LUPUS (304) £280, 9/47 CERES (27) £750, 9/47 POLARIS (334) £375.

RIVER SEVERN CATCHMENT BOARD 9/43 VENUS (95) & MERAK (312), £1,000

H. DEAN & SON, MANCHESTER 4/47 COLUMBA (29) £450 & 7/47 URANUS (380), £400 (Both boats subsequently passed to John Knill)

THOMAS CLAYTON (PADDINGTON) LIMITED 9/43 ADELAIDE (204), ALBERT (205), ALEXANDRA (206), ANNE (212) for use in waste disposal work.

GRAND UNION CANAL COMPANY In 1942 five boats were requisitioned by the Ministry of War Transport and shortened to become ice breakers but later they were returned to the GUC and entered the maintenance fleet. SEXTANS (83), SICKLE (84), THEOPHILUS (91), TYCHO (93), RENTON (164) 30/9/42 LEONIDS (301), REGULUS (343), SARPEDON (350), SCALES (353), THEA (372), THOTH (373), TRIAGULUM (378) £3,000; four to be fitted up as hand dredgers and three for conversion to pumping boats. 30/11/45 ARCHIMEDES (12) £403, CEPHEUS (26) £379, CORONA (32) £406, DUKE (38) £183, EDWARD (39) £188, HENRY (49) £191, MERCURY (60) £383, PLANET (72) £391, PRINCE (78) £258, VICTORIA (97) £177, BILSTER (118) £483, CORVUS (260) £253, SATURN (352) £205, TAURUS (370) £281

Whilst many GUCCC boats still survive and are lovingly cared for by their owners, some were not so lucky. BARRHEAD, one of the wooden butties built by Walkers at Rickmansworth, is shown languishing derelict in a backwater of the River Stort at Sawbridgeworth. (Author's collection)